Jonny Baker works for the Chur
and supporting mission and new ways
emerging culture in the UK. This involves encouraging, com...
ing, networking and training mission and pioneer leaders. He is
a member of Grace, an alternative worship community in London,
where he has curated many worship experiences. He has authored
the book *Alternative Worship*, which is a collection of liturgical
resources for the church year, and contributed to the books *Mass
Culture* and *The Rite Stuff*. He co-ordinated worship for Greenbelt
Arts Festival for several years. He has been involved in various
creative arts and worship projects in the UK and internationally,
the most successful of which has been the Labyrinth, which he
helped design, first installed in St Paul's Cathedral. He runs <www.
proost.co.uk>, a creative company that produces inspiring resources
that fuel faith. He is a London Independent Photographer, and
blogs at <http://jonnybaker.blogs.com>.

CURATING WORSHIP

Jonny Baker

First published in Great Britain in 2010

Society for Promoting Christian Knowledge
36 Causton Street
London SW1P 4ST
www.spckpublishing.co.uk

British Library Cataloguing-in-Publication Data
A catalogue record for this book is available from the British Library

ISBN 978–0–281–06235–5

1 3 5 7 9 10 8 6 4 2

Typeset by Graphicraft Ltd, Hong Kong
Printed in Great Britain by Ashford Colour Press

Produced on paper from sustainable forests

To those who have the gift of not fitting in

'The new paradigm begins as soon as you are ready to perceive it.'
Kate Tempest

Contents

Contents

Contributors

Steve Collins is a member of Grace alternative worship community – <www.freshworship.org> – and lives in Ealing, west London. He is an architect specializing in corporate interiors, and works for a large practice in central London a couple of blocks behind Tate Modern. He has contributed online through various websites: <www.smallfire.org>, for an amazing collection of photos of alternative worship events; <www.smallritual.org> for personal reflections; <www.alternativeworship.org>, the directory site for alternative worship. He blogs at <www.smallritual.blogs.com/small_ritual>.

Laura Drane is one of the founding members of Sanctus1 – <www.sanctus1.co.uk> – an emerging church in Manchester city centre, as part of which she's been planning and curating services since 2002. She works in the arts and cultural sectors as a project manager and consultant, particularly specializing in festivals.

Ana Draper is a doctor in systems therapy and works as a consultant psychotherapist in the palliative care field. She started to wander and explore as a child in the jungles of Ecuador, where she walked a path from which she witnessed inequality, poverty, and barriers to education and health care. This formed a hunger in her stomach to feed the poor and to work towards a world of inclusion. She then moved to England and experienced a whole new world, got socio-vertigo and spent some years trying to recover, although it is always now in her DNA. In this time she joined other travellers in an exploration of a whole new terrain, where faith became about questions and doubt and she was able to connect with her childhood hunger. As she journeyed and explored new places, she started to reach out to those marginalized by spiritual cliques that turned people into clones. She strived to create freedom that allowed others to celebrate and explore what it means to be human and yet made in the image of God. This has involved founding and being part of different communities along the way, including Live On Planet Earth in Kent, L8r and Shape in Northwood.

Nic Hughes is a designer, lecturer and co-founder of Vaux – <www.vaux.net>. He blogs at <http://hauntedgeographies.typepad.com>. **Kester Brewin** co-founded Vaux and is a teacher and freelance writer. His second book, *Other: Loving Self, God and Neighbour in a World of Fractures*, is published by Hodder. Kester blogs at <www.kesterbrewin.com>.

Cheryl Lawrie lives in inner-city Melbourne and is generously employed by the Uniting Church in Australia to spend her time exploring the city to find the meeting points between spirituality, culture and context. She has curated many events in the city with a collective and she also curates worship in a prison. She regularly writes for the *Age* newspaper on spirituality and postmodern culture, and would one day love to be a landscape gardener. Her online hub is <http://holdthisspace.org.au>.

Lilly Lewin is a worship curator, atmosphere architect, author, speaker and extroverted contemplative. She is the co-founder and curator of Thinplace and Maproom in Cincinnati, Ohio where she lives with husband Rob and sons Mac and Hudson and the wonder spaniel. Thinplace is a community of friends seeking to live their faith in the way of Jesus with monthly and weekly gatherings featuring Lectio Divina, artistic response, journalling and hospitality. Maproom is an experiential open house for God for college and post-college adults in and around the University of Cincinnati. She is the author of *Sacred Space* with Dan Kimball (Zondervan, 2008).

Sonia and Iain Mainstone-Cotton and **Clare Birch** were founders of Sanctuary in Bath. Born out of friendships and a desire to meet with God, Sanctuary started when several people who were having trouble finding space to worship in mainstream church decided to begin meeting together and exploring worship, faith and creativity in ways that felt authentic. It began with a monthly worship service, and later a monthly teaching/discussion slot and a monthly community meal were added. In the 11 years since Sanctuary started, children have arrived, and lots of people have come and gone, but the essence of Sanctuary remains the same – creating spaces where people can meet with God, have fun with that process, and learn to love one another – <http://sanctuarybath.wordpress.com>. Clare is a jeweller and writer and currently works in a community café. Iain is a stonecarver, lettering artist and sculptor – <www.iaincotton.co.uk>. Sonia is a charity development worker and an early years trainer and consultant.

Martin Poole has been an ordained, non-stipendiary priest in the Church of England since 1987 when he was working as a professional actor and serving in a south London parish with John Sentamu. Since then he has become a TV marketing professional working on branding and marketing strategy for clients such as ITV, Sky and the BBC and most recently setting up his own international consultancy, Sway Media. He moved to Brighton and Hove in 1999 and in 2007 set up BEYOND – <www.beyondchurch.co.uk> – with a dedicated group of like-minded volunteers and some resource funding from the Chichester diocese. BEYOND has a growing reputation for its creative worship installations and journeys in public spaces, the best known of which is the Beach Hut Advent Calendar.

Pete Rollins and **Jonny McEwen** are active participants in Ikon – <www.ikon.org.uk>, a Belfast-based collective which offers anarchic experiments in transformance art. Jonny is an artist with a background in creative approaches to conflict. He also produces chilled out music under the name Dubh – see <www.proost.co.uk>. Pete is a writer, lecturer, storyteller and public speaker. His virtual study is <http://peterrollins.net>.

Steve Taylor has led churches, both as a church planter and change agent pastor. He is now a Kiwi-in-exile, working as Director of Missiology, Uniting College, Adelaide. He has a PhD in emerging church and cultural change, is the author of *The Out of Bounds Church?* (Zondervan, 2005) and blogs at <www.emergentkiwi. org.nz>.

Sue Wallace is a musician and multimedia artist who has been working for the Visions alternative worship community since 1992 – <www.visions-york.org>. She was ordained as a Church of England priest in 2006 and has written four books on multi-sensory prayer which have been inspired by ideas used in the Visions services over the years. Transcendence has been a recent partnership between Visions and York Minster curating an ancient-future mass in the context of a cathedral.

Dave White curates Stations of the Cross in the public gardens in Hamilton, New Zealand – <www.stations.org.nz>. He works in mission with Incedo – <http://incedo.org.nz> – is a writer and is part of Exile, an alternative worship community in Hamilton.

Introduction

Curation is a term that comes from the art world. The curator is the person who has the role of imagining and overseeing an exhibition in a gallery or museum. This includes working with an artist or group of artists, selecting and commissioning which pieces of work to display, and arranging those in the spaces. The curator may also be the person who looks after a museum's collection, the 'keeper', which is what the role meant more traditionally. When you visit an exhibition it is highly unlikely that you will see the curator there or even be aware that there is one unless you read the small print in the catalogue. That is a sign of good curation – if the work is done well the curator disappears behind it.[1] The curator's role takes place over months and sometimes years before you arrive. But by the time you are there it is done. The environment has been created, the art has been framed and an articulation has been made. If it has been done well, it is a space that can be navigated seamlessly and visitors can immerse themselves in it without giving a second thought to the curator. As the art is encountered there are moments of epiphany, delight, provocation, questions are evoked and the work of the artist or artists on display is appreciated more. If it's been good it can linger in the imagination. The catalogue, if there is one, is an integral extension of the exhibition and can be taken away to explore further beyond the experience itself to find more depth.

Worship curation takes this approach as a model for how worship is put together. It affords a very different way of thinking about what is involved in leading worship and what it means. It throws up in the air whether leadership is even a good word to use. It certainly imagines a very different kind of leadership, which is backstage rather than on stage. Worship leading generally seems to have come to mean one of two things: either the role of the president or person who presides over liturgy in a denominational church, or the role of a charismatic personality who fronts a worship band. One way of thinking about both of these is as genres. They have a certain discourse, a logic, known rules of engagement and sets of expectations to them within which the leader and congregation know how to operate. That is a good thing. Genres in films or books function like that in our lives. If you mess with a genre or mix genres it generally doesn't work very well. There is an art to leading in both of these genres that can be done in creative and interesting ways. Some people are very skilful and gifted at it. Curation is a very different genre. It blows apart the notion of someone up front leading, and opens up a very different kind of imagination. Curation is a term that is being adopted in a number of areas beyond the discipline of the art world, not just in worship. The *New York Times* picked up on this observation.[2] This is because it affords this very rich and different way of thinking about leadership. A worship curator makes a context and a frame for worship, arranging elements in it. The content is provided by other people.[3]

Curating Worship is in two parts. The first explores curation both in the art world and in worship, considering the kind of imagination, process, skills and discipline that are involved – what might make for good curation. The second and major part of the book is a series of interviews and conversations with worship curators from a number of contexts and communities who have constructed amazing worship experiences. These can be read in any order. This approach grew out of the movement known as Alternative Worship[4] and most of the people interviewed were or are part of it. That term is not in and of itself important. Its insights and inspiration have now been picked up and co-opted and remixed in lots of other contexts. The book is inspired in part by Hans Obrist, who feared the loss of memory of some of the practices of curation in the art world and published a series of interviews, *A Brief History of Curating*,[5] teasing out from curators the ideas and theories behind their approach, and the practical processes involved. I hope these interviews in a similar way help avoid amnesia and provide sparks of imagination. They also highlight how the new electronic information environment enables rich networking, connectivity and sharing of ideas and learning across the world.

Part 1

CURATION IN THE ART WORLD AND IN WORSHIP

A space for encounter

Somehow, something happens. Sometimes that's hard to remember when you're taping down cords or lighting coals or dashing down the hall to the photocopier (again).

Somehow, something happens. People gather. And in silence and words. Sound and movement. Stillness. Between the clumsiness and the elegance and the whimsy and the beauty. Somewhere, there, something happens.

And that's the grace of it. That's the Life in it. That's the hope for it.

A space for allowing our humanity to be held gently. A space for wonder. A space to be at home. A space for lamenting. A space for hoping. A space for playing. A space for encounter.[1]

In an old disused church in Bermondsey at Dilston Grove a pool is filled a few feet deep with black water. On the edge are some steps up and one solitary stepping stone. It's inviting someone to step out from the edge and see what happens. This is the Bridge, an installation by Michael Cross.[2] It's actually a trial, a prototype for something he hopes will be on a bigger scale on a lake. The way it works is that when you take the risk of stepping out, the force of your weight on the stepping stone triggers another one to appear from underneath the water. In this way the viewer slowly leaves the edge one step at a time to make their way out into the water. It's a wonderful location for it. And it is nerve-racking. That experience lingered with me for quite some time. For several weeks, when I prayed I could picture that step of faith and trust.

One of the most memorable exhibitions I think I have ever been to was *New Ocean* by Doug Aitken at the Serpentine Gallery.

He is an artist who works in film and photography. The journey through the exhibition began in the basement with a film and recorded sound of ice cracking. Writing about it seems somehow too far removed from the experience but I found I was moved to tears standing listening as the coldness and hardness cracked. It was particularly the sound. The exhibition then took you through several film installations. These were layered narratives of people in busy city lives who were on the train to work, or running down a corridor, and they would all shift between the urban pressure to a slowed-down or quiet movement that felt like breathing. This was something simple, like focusing on the gentle closing of eyes in an almost meditative fashion or a graceful gymnast in slow motion. In one sequence a man running home from work ended up lying on the floor in a wilderness, collapsed but somehow peaceful. This multi-layered set of sequences moved me to reflect on living in fast-paced city life, to pause and reflect on where the spaces of solitude and quiet and prayer are in the city, when travelling on the Underground. The journey ended in the upstairs room, which is a lovely round space at the Serpentine. The sound of rushing water filled the air; projected all around were waterfalls and overhead a projection of the ocean from beneath the surface. There was a sequence of someone falling into the water. It was like being immersed. This was such a renewing and healing sensation. I obviously bring my own self and stories and interpretations to the art but I was prayerfully asking for God to immerse me in Godself in a new way, to renew me. I stayed in the space a long time and went away changed, slowed down. What struck me about this exhibition wasn't just that I loved some of the works of the artist. It was also the way that the art used the context of the building, and that the journey through the art, while subtle, had a wonderful flow and development to it. It was brilliantly curated.

On Carnaby Street busy shoppers are rushing to get ready for Christmas. They race past a strange-looking store adorned with spray paint and camouflage netting and graffiti. This is Santa's

Ghetto, which pulls together a collective of street artists who take over a store in London for a few weeks in the run-up to Christmas. Its deconstructed underground feel, set in the context of the glittery Christmas decorations all around, is just the perfect location. This is a different kind of experience – designed to shock, to pull a rug from under the feet of consumer Christmas. Banksy has a piece there, set in a stable but Jesus is stencilled onto a huge piece of cardboard – crucified but holding in his outstretched hands bags of shopping. This image provokes, asks questions, unmasks. One of the images that most lingered in my mind was a piece called *Liberty Shame*. The image is of the Statue of Liberty holding her face in her hands in shame. The way this is put together is brilliant. Context here makes it. It just wouldn't work in a nice gallery or museum. And the arrangement and décor enhance the underground street feel of the art.

The Tate Modern Turbine Hall is a huge space. Every six months an artist fills the space with an installation. It is an incredible challenge. They have pretty much all been brilliant in their own way. *How It Is* by Balka occupies the space at the time I am writing this. It is a huge container that has black walls, floor and ceiling. It is a void, a room of darkness. If you arrive and go straight into it, because your eyes have not had time to adjust it's impossible to see anything, though you can hear voices of other people in the darkness. I entered with hands in front of me and gradually made my way to the back. I then turned around; gradually my eyes began to adjust to the darkness and I could make out other people, and looking back see the light of the entrance. After ten minutes it really didn't seem so dark or fearful at all. The write-up on the installation, by the artist or curator, says this:

How shall I move forward? You might ask yourself as you stand at the threshold, confronted by the darkness ahead. The unknown can be terrifying, especially if it is also without light. How you approach it is unique, as your first encounter with anything can only ever be as an individual. Staring ahead into the black void may make you wonder whether to move ahead at all.

It's one thing to think about an experience like this but actually navigating it is so much more evocative. I imagine people have reflected on all sorts of unknowns they face as they have walked into the darkness. I found myself thinking about my work and life's direction, as I have recently taken on a new role and it feels at times a bit like going into the unknown. But it was reassuring to think that the unknown began to be less dark and fearful than it seemed at first. I was also thinking about the darkness of God, the starlit darkness.

I feel spoilt, living in London where there is so much amazing art. These spaces are experiential, contemplative, spaces of encounter, spaces to change speed. Galleries and museums are one of the few public spaces where people in cities slow down and reflect, where slowness and silence can flourish. Equally, where artists and curators take art into public spaces the same effects can be received. Antony Gormley's astonishing installation of around 100 life-size sculpted figures, staring out to the ocean, spread along a stretch of sand on Crosby beach near Liverpool, is a great example.

Art can do different things, have different effects. At times it evokes wonder. Every year I go to the Wildlife Photographer of the Year exhibition for a dose of wonder. Other times it is simply a different kind of space. At times it provokes questions, evokes grief, and can be difficult to take – it certainly shouldn't always be comfortable. As a Christian I find these spaces spiritual, prayerful: places to encounter God. They move me and touch my soul. And I find that experiences tend to linger for a long time in the memory rather than be gone in a moment. They communicate at a depth. I have had many moments of epiphany.[3] This is part of what makes a great exhibition. The curator makes exhibitions as spaces for experience.[4] The curator enables connections and communication to take place between artists, art and the public without getting in the way. There is a place for educating the public in a particular artist's work and how that is located in the tradition, but the best curators tend to let the art speak for itself so that viewers can look and look and look again and immerse themselves in the experience. Exhibitions where the viewers spend all the time reading the explanations have generally got the balance wrong.[5] People can follow up on the artist afterwards through the catalogue or online.

Worship curation, drawing inspiration from the world of contemporary art, creates spaces: for encounter, for experience, for reflection, to change speeds, for prayer, for questions, for exploration, for meditation, for provocation, for moments of epiphany. Creativity and imagination are brought to bear to open up encounters between God, art, worship and the people. Lots of examples in both public spaces and church spaces are explored through the book in the interviews.

Part of the motivation for writing this book and conducting interviews with practitioners is that creative processes can seem mysterious and unattainable, even intimidating. The hope is that lifting the lid off the process and thinking might help demystify curating worship, and encourage people: 'You can do it!' Most of the communities involved in curating worship are not populated by professional artists. Their currency is the power of ideas, cultivating environments where creativity can flourish, rather than technical skills or artistry – although if those gifts are available in the community then obviously they will be welcomed, and by getting involved in this sort of worship artistry certainly does develop. Most of the worship is done with the resources that are to hand rather than on large budgets.

There isn't one way to curate worship – the interviews demonstrate that. Some groups spend a year on a project, others have two planning sessions and then leave it to people to create the content. Some have a large group involved in planning, while others work in small teams. Some are worshipping communities and others are more like art collectives.

Grace is the Christian community I belong to. It's a creative congregation of an Anglican church, and has been part of the alternative worship movement in the UK. We generally work in small teams, planning around 12 worship events a year. Typically someone might curate a worship service once or twice in the year and get involved in a team at four or five events. Some people don't ever get involved in any, though – it's not their thing! We'll often manage to plan with just two meetings, and people then work on their contributions. We don't rehearse or look at contributions in advance, as we like to retain the rough edges and the element of surprise at what people bring. Curating worship requires a set of instincts, skills and mindset that is different from other ways of leading worship. There are quite a number of considerations to hold together. It can get complex. For this reason, in Grace we wrote some practical guidelines and considerations for people taking the curation role. These make the task look more like project management, and are pragmatic rather than theoretical. I have included these guidelines in the Appendix because it's probably helpful to see curation at this practical level, as well as at the level of ideas articulation, negotiation and world-making, explored in the next chapter.

One of the main differences between curators in the art world and worship curation is that the norm in worship is to work in creative teams. The task is to enable a group to develop something creative together rather than to realize their own personal vision. That isn't always easy, particularly if you naturally want to control things. Nic Hughes reflects in our interview on his journey from having a very controlling approach in the early days of Vaux to arriving at a place where open source principles apply, particularly that 'whoever comes is the right people'. At the heart of this is trust. A curator needs to operate on the basis of trust: trust of the process, trust of the people who are the creative team, trust of the community, trust in the institutions and relationships that the community is located in, trust of the people who come, that they will do what they need to do and receive what they need to receive, trust that there will be moments of epiphany, trust that God will indwell what has been created. The curator's posture is best when he or she is able to hold open the space for ideas and contributions generously rather than acting as a control filter. The approaches curators may take can be described in many ways: as a midwife, helping bring something to birth out of the community, as a DJ, remixing and sampling out of the tradition and ideas, as a broker of opportunities, as a fool who looks for the craziest ideas and dares to believe they can be realized, as a middlewoman acting as a negotiator between artists and institutions, as a permission giver, as an encourager who has learned how to nudge and swerve things in new directions, as a magpie making do from what is to hand. Curators are contextual. They are happy out of the way rather than in the spotlight. They are creators of environments. They are hard workers who will go the extra mile to make things happen. And they are amateurs, who do it for love not money. Above all they are lovers – lovers of God, of worship, of creativity, of the tradition, of people, of their culture.

Making a world

Worship imagines a world, nothing less. In curating worship perhaps the single most important question is what kind of a world is imagined, made, constructed. Simon Sheikh[1] suggests, in relation to exhibition-making, that if the curator is happy with the way the world is now they should continue to create exhibitions as always, repeating formats and circulations. But if they are not content with the world they are in, and the art world, then they will have to produce other exhibitions. This is a very resonant idea. Restlessness is a sure sign that the world being made by other imaginaries doesn't ring true and that a counter-imagination is called for. Worship curation is not simply about stylistic difference, a bit of creativity and tweaking around the edges. It cuts deeper. As illustrated by the interviews in the second half of the book, it is and has been about imagining new worlds, new relationships, new strategies and tactics, and counter-publics, about saying that other worlds are possible, that business as usual in the church, in worship, in theology, in consumer culture, in the world at large, in life, simply will not do.

This world-making, or terra-forming,[2] involves articulation, imagination and continuity.[3]

> A work of art is at best an articulation of something as much as it is a representation of someone: it is a proposal for how things could be seen, an offering but not a handout. Articulation is the formulation of your position and politics, where you are and where you want to go, as well as a concept of companionship: you can come along or not.[4]

It's interesting to rework this quote from Sheikh replacing 'art' with 'worship'. Worship is an articulation of something, of how things

10

could be seen. A community or a curator has a vision, a take, something to articulate. It might not be fully worked out but it is not neutral. There is a lot of pretence around being neutral but one of the gifts of postmodern culture has been to make us suspicious of anyone making such a claim. When we celebrate communion in Grace, in most of our liturgies we articulate a radical vision of hospitality and welcome around the table – this is deliberately in the face of and counter to the imagination of a world where only insiders are welcomed. So, for example, in a song we have written, 'Table of Christ', one of the lines is 'Come if the church stops you at the door'. Articulation is also around subtle things like deconstructing the front, or the role of the expert or priest (or not), around posture and layout, and around the use of culture and popular culture in worship – making a world out of the stuff of everyday life rather than articulating a world that runs in parallel to the rest of life.

Art rarely works when it shouts – maybe punk is the exception?! – and worship is the same. So the notion of articulation as an offering rather than a handout, an invitation rather than an instruction,[5] or being evocative rather than descriptive[6] sits much more in tune with the cultural sensibilities and the genre. It's good to have clarity about what is being articulated but to offer and explore rather than shout and dictate. Tone and a humble posture are really important. I recently went to an exhibition of photos of Afghanistan. They were beautiful, but in the end I disliked them. I was angry because there were simply too many photos with an agenda of the Dutch Army – who had commissioned the work – being heroic. The curator could have articulated this differently. Many of the worship experiences described in the interviews have multiple layers and meanings, so people can find a number of pathways through. But they still have articulation.

The gift of imagination is part of what marks us out as human beings. It's what it means to imagine God. It's an incredible gift. Curating is a process with imagination and creativity. It's the fun part! At a macro level it's about ways of seeing, imagining another world. But it's also about the process of coming up with ideas and dreaming things that have not been done before or have a different take. I explore this process with several people in the interviews but it's hard to tease out where ideas come from and how groups cultivate an environment of creativity. But it is that environment that is key. A certain level of chaos, food and drink, and learning to entertain the craziest suggestions – all are part of the heady mix. In many church circles the only gifts that are valued for worship are musical ones (and even then of a small range of music) or the ability to speak well (preferably in a good English accent). This attitude needs shattering, and opening up so that poets, photographers, ideas people, geeks, theologians, liturgists, designers, writers, cooks, politicians, architects, moviemakers, storytellers, parents, campaigners, children, bloggers, DJs, VJs, craft-makers, or just anybody who comes and is willing to bounce ideas around, can get involved. It's so exciting to be part of making and producing in this way. I like to think sometimes that the angels sit nearby, in the rafters or on the balcony, thinking, what on earth are these crazy people going to do in worship today? And they keep getting surprised and smiles are brought to their faces. Who would have thought of Beach Hut Advent Calendars, Stations of the Cross in public gardens, embedding prayers in slabs of concrete, a holy space in a car park basement, slapping containers of installations in city centres, sending surprises through the post, welcomers dressed in contamination suits, guerrilla worship, and children participating creatively with adults? These are all things mentioned by the people interviewed in the second half of the book. I love what has been dreamed, and is yet to be dreamed. Creativity is a muscle that can be developed – it needs to be flexed. For some people it has gone flabby through underuse, but there's nothing better for it than being around other people flexing their imagination. It's a habit that can be caught through being in a creative environment.

Imagination is not just about the artistic content and arrangement. It's about the whole process. A museum director's first task is to create a public[7] – not just to do great shows, but to create an audience that trusts the institution. I suspect that a lot of people who curate worship are most interested in the creative process – that's where the imaginative work is done. I have been to many events and installations that are wonderfully creative, but only a very small group have been fortunate enough to find them. It's good to apply the same level of imagination to create a public as it is to the event/experience itself.

Art and worship both have a narrative or a history, depending on who does the telling. There is a tradition, a line of ancestry, a communion of artists and saints worldwide and down the ages. To curate is to be located in this line – sometimes straight, other times kicking off from, subverting, giving a new spin to, and opening up the traditions. It's how traditions get remade and taken forward. The beauty of the art and church worlds is that there is so much to play with down the ages and across the globe. This is continuity, even if sometimes a rupture is brought to that continuity. Being located in a particular denomination or stream affords certain rules or grammar within which to curate, with accompanying treasures to take out of the cupboard of tradition. If you are outside of that, continuity will play out slightly differently. So a big consideration for curators is how they are located in relation to continuity of the worlds before and the world to come. Alternative worship in this respect was always more keen on stressing continuity and location in tradition in contrast with the modernizing moves of worship in the 1970s and 1980s.

In the literature and debates around curation it's fascinating seeing the themes that surface on a regular basis. One is the challenge of negotiating newness in art in the midst of the public, artists, museums, galleries, benefactors and patrons, and the range of institutions and powers at play in the art world. In short, the curator is most definitely a negotiator, a middleman or middle-woman,[8] even if that wasn't what they signed up for.

Some curators locate themselves at the independent freelance end of things so they have the creative space to fulfil their vision.

They problematize the institutions of the art world – they haven't got time for them. So Seth Siegelaub[9] calls the museum 'a cemetery for art' with its focus on historicization, and criticizes its vested social and structural interests. He suggests that one problem is that art institutions can be very detached from artists, so there's no point bothering with them.

On the other hand there are plenty who have taken roles inside museums and use them to negotiate permissions for artists to do amazing things in and around those huge spaces. This is often while they recognize the need for deep institutional change. Robert Storr of MOMA reflects on how curators may once have been among those criticizing the institutions but now find themselves on the inside of the establishment and only have themselves to blame if the tradition is not renewed – 'If the art world is not responsive to the needs and achievements of artists there are all kinds of people to blame for that but mostly we must blame ourselves'[10] – and he appeals for working creatively with the institutions rather than reactively against them.

Those curators who have managed to create the most impact in and around museums have managed to develop or maintain closeness to artists alongside the ability to create trust in the interplay between the institution, the public and the artists. Without that trust it's hard to achieve much, but once it is in place amazing things are possible. For example, Willem Sandberg[11] talked about the courage to run a museum in a non-academic experimental way. That simply isn't possible without a lot of graft in building trust.

There have been a couple of significant changes in museums in particular. One was that museums stopped seeing themselves as just showing permanent collections, and used the artworks in their possession to create different kinds of themed shows, bringing the best stuff out only from time to time, showing it in different ways, making specific articulations and connections. And the second was a shift such that some museums began to see themselves as sites for experimentation; they said goodbye to their isolation and function as 'an aesthetic church'.[12] Out of this emerged the idea of the museum as a workshop or laboratory or even as a space of risk.

Many of the museums and galleries in London seem to have embraced this ethos. I remember going to an amazing evening run by the contemporary art collective Onedotzero at the Victoria and Albert Museum. DJs, projections and installations in traditional spaces had this playful laboratory feel.

The same kinds of debates take place in relation to the wonderfully creative mission leaders, improvisers and worship curators who have been part of the emerging church and alternative worship movements that have subverted, shaken, deconstructed and brought newness to the Christian faith in the soil of postmodern cultures, both at the edges and in the heart of the institutions. I think continuity is best thought of as 'both/and' or 'centre/ edge'. I love it that there are curators who want to sail off the edge and do things that the institution cannot imagine or permit. And I also love it that there are those who patiently earn trust and negotiate space within the heart of the church. The beauty of the new environment is that it's so easy for those people to connect and share their learning and stories and journey together. Many of those I interview later in the book have negotiated space within institutions with varying degrees of how much on the edge they are. Sue Wallace has negotiated space within York Minster for Transcendence and describes the creative negotiations born of trust. Equally Ikon and Vaux have pushed the envelope precisely by moving more to the edges and 'curating beyond the canon'. I came across the notion of curating beyond the canon through curator Okwui Enwezor – although it sounds like something you would find in a book on Anglican liturgy. He says:

I have always tried to work outside the canon and do it within culture. This is not to say that the canon is bad but that the canon already has a highly circumscribed notion of what artistic practice could be. I think it is already embedded

15

within a very large historical determination that is in many ways very much set. It is un-giving. I am really interested in curating within culture, even when I am drawing from the canon in order to unsettle the kind of methodological issues that have become so situated in one place. To curate within culture is to take a space of culture in the present as an open place of working and that means that you have a greater mobility in terms of bringing in procedures of making art that may not have a place in the broader context of contemporary art. I suppose this is the realm within which most curators work except when their ambitions change and they want to make an exhibition of Andy Warhol. What could be more generic? When their ambitions change, when they want to become more institutionalised, they want to prove their commitment to the canon. This is what usually happens, it is more strategic. You can see immediately the intellectual poverty of some of those gestures and I completely understand what you see when the move happens. The curators have already reached a threshold when they want to have a permanent job.[13]

There are a number of ways that worship might be curated beyond the canon (and again it reads well to replace 'art' with 'worship' in that paragraph).

There has been a growing edge of moving things into public spaces within culture, closing the gap between worship and life – art installations such as the Beach Hut Advent Calendar and Stations of the Cross, worship in cafés and bars and proximity spaces.

Curators in the early days of alternative worship discovered contextual, feminist, liberation and black theologies that were seemingly beyond the canon, at least of their own tradition or starting point. Listening to voices from other contexts exposes where the canon is read from, through whose eyes, with the idea that it is simply a perspective rather than the final word. This opened up the possibility of doing contextual theology[14] and reading with postmodern eyes.

The content of particular experiences being curated might push the boundaries. This might be something simple such as the articulation of liturgy or the use of technology and culture in worship: Mac Classics on the holy table or Discmans in St Paul's Cathedral – playful, messing with things, matter out of place. In the interview with Nic and Kester I discuss a Vaux service on the theme of 'dirt', which included throwing the communion bread and wine dramatically, daring to mess with 'sacred' things.

At a panel on curating worship I conducted at Greenbelt, a couple of people were there from the Joint Liturgical Commission of the Church of England. A discussion arose around what permissions there actually are to be creative in that tradition. The answer given was that the Commissioners were wanting to encourage the kind of creative approach to worship being discussed and practised. But they were frustrated that they are perceived as the liturgical 'thought police' who are waiting to pounce on anyone who doesn't abide by the rules! There is a strange myth that correct liturgy is recited by rote rather than with a creative and imaginative articulation in a frame that draws on the deep wells of the tradition. It's such a dull and stagnant view. The 'canon' is sometimes nothing more than a perceived set of boundaries in people's imagination. Curating beyond the canon is precisely the kind of tactic that will lead to renewal.

There was a small booklet produced off the back of a Lambeth conference[15] that tried to address this issue in the Anglican Communion globally. The motivation behind this document was that the 'canon' was a Western set of liturgies and so it sought to encourage and give permission for contextual or inculturated liturgies. These two quotes give a flavour of this truly remarkable statement:

Our lack of inculturation has fostered both the alienation of some Christians and an over ready willingness of others to live in two different cultures, one of their religion and and the other of their everyday life. Other Christians again have left our churches because of this cultural insensitivity. Similarly non Christians have found the foreignness of the church a great barrier to faith.

True inculturation implies a willingness in worship to listen to culture . . . it has to make contact with the deep feelings of people. It can only be achieved through an openness to innovation and experimentation, an encouragement of local creativity, and a readiness to reflect critically at every stage of the process, a process which in principle is never ending.

As in many mission issues, the Church has had to think about this in relation to global contexts but has only latterly realized that the same issues are pertinent in our own cultures. Worship curators and artists will lead the way in this sort of innovation and experimentation.

Part 2

INTERVIEWS BY
JONNY BAKER

Treating church as a design problem

STEVE COLLINS

———•◆•———

Jonny: Steve, we live in London – such a fantastic city for art and culture. We have been to a number of exhibitions together over the years. For example, I remember a group of us from Grace going to one at the Hayward Gallery on kinetic art, which really inspired us. We'd often say that we were doing the same kinds of things only on a much cheaper budget! And we'd often say that some of the meanings we were opening up had as much thought in them as the things we encountered in these big galleries. How do you think this connection between contemporary art installations and alternative worship came about?

Steve: A major part of the original brief for alternative worship was cultural (re)connection, and that meant engaging with the arts of all kinds, and making a space for artists to work within the Church in a context of experimentation and permission. The idea was both to read where society was at, through the arts, and to speak to society as Christians, through the arts. So the artists came and did their stuff, bringing their cultural connections with them.

But alternative worship in the UK coincided with a powerful and vital new movement in contemporary art among people of the same age and cultural background. The new movement was above all conceptual and installation-based. What counted was not technical skill or craft, although these were often of a high order, but communication of ideas, in a language taken directly from contemporary life and the media, and using the stuff of everyday life – ashtrays, tights, TVs, bedding, booze.

21

These communicative environments provided one answer to the conundrum, how do we communicate in church without doing a sermon? Without being dominated by words?

They also showed us how to make art, and how to communicate ideas, cheaply, even by using trash and dirt. We saw how humble materials could stack up into something profound – could be redeemed. We saw how viewers could interact with art, physically and conceptually, making their own meanings and making (or unmaking) the art. We saw that art could be, literally, liturgy – a work of the people. We saw that art could be made by editing, whether from the stuff around us or from audience contributions, however unskilled. We saw that the meaning of art could be in (inter)actions and sensual impact, not just analysis or observation.

So the British art world of the last 20 years has been and continues to be a masterclass in worship techniques! I think we'd have struggled if it had been all about painting, for example. Do you believe in coincidence?

J: In retrospect what you are saying seems obvious, but I'm not sure how intentional it was at the time. Were there particular exhibitions in contemporary art, or artists that particularly influenced the ideas you have brought to developing these communicative environments in worship?

In what sense has being an architect helped your approach to curation? Presumably being an architect has a disciplined way of imagining how spaces are created and used. Looking at some of your pieces on <www.smallritual.org> there is a playful re-imagining of church environment in lots of them, whether as round the table, in the city, in networks, or a completely redesigned space that has to be small and doesn't allow large gatherings. A big part of the role of curation is thinking about space and environment and how individual pieces that artists produce are going to fit in the flow of the space and what the interplay between them will be, either physically or in the sense of creating a narrative flow in time. Vaux describe themselves as worship architects on their publicity, I seem to remember. Perhaps you truly are a worship architect? I'm sure it feels very intuitive but can you reflect a bit on your way of seeing, of imagining in relation to space and environment?

S: I don't think it was very intentional either! We were magpies, picking up things that might be useful, groping our way forward in alt worship as they were groping their way forward in art. Some art stuff that sticks with me:

- Self Storage[1] – 1995, Royal College of Art students curated by Brian Eno and Laurie Anderson. Walking miles through a labyrinthine self-storage warehouse in Wembley to discover little installations in some of the units – all sorts of random stuff. So big it took a couple of hours to walk round.
- HG[2] – also 1995, in Clink Street vaults when they were derelict. You were met outside in the street, and invited to step through a small door, not knowing what was inside, and found yourself in an Edwardian dining room from which the inhabitants had seemingly fled halfway through a meal. No explanation, but opening the other door leads to a mysterious journey through incredibly elaborate set pieces.
- Mike Nelson's installations – like HG, you step through a door and find yourself in the rooms and corridors of an alternative world, with no explanation. You end up scrutinizing every object for clues, and some of it means something and some of it is just scene-setting.

So all of these have the narrative trail, picking up clues, not quite knowing what's trash and what's art or what's around the next corner. They show how disparate pieces and incidents can be strung together as a journey. They use the stuff of the 'real' world – real chairs and bottles and clocks and newspapers – sourced, not made. They show how to construct meaning with everyday or available things. Brian Eno: 'that's the real idea of Self Storage: to take a vulgar, secular space and charge it in some way. It's meant to say to people: you can do it, too . . . it's really not that hard.'[3]

Regarding curation as an architect, it's my editorial skills that are required more than my spatial skills. The way we create services at Grace means that we generally don't know what the parts look like or how big they are in advance, so spatial arrangements tend to happen on the night, apart from the occasional set piece. But a large part of the designer's skill is in editing ideas and forms to produce coherence and meaning.

To step back a little, design (architectural or otherwise) is about problem-solving. The designer starts by analysis and questioning. What do the clients want? What do they need (may not be the same thing)? What do they really want and need (they may not understand their desires and situations)? How do time and budget constrain possible outcomes? And so on, in depth. The synthesis of new forms comes after analysis, and demonstrates how well the designer has understood the task – including the unspoken aspects.

There is a story, which may be apocryphal, that a client came to Norman Foster for a new factory, and he redesigned their manufacturing process so that they could stay in their old one. What that means is that in order to design a new factory Foster had to examine very thoroughly the client's existing processes and organization. And in this case, he saw that improvements could be made which would remove the need for a new building. Note that the client had not seen this – the designer has the advantage of detachment. The designer also looks at the wider context: other people's solutions to similar problems, changes on the horizon in technology or regulation, changes in society that will affect how people work or dwell – all this has to be weighed. Architecture is generally trying to be a little in the future, to avoid being instantly out of date. Sometimes architects aim for a future that doesn't happen. When appraising architecture, always ask yourself what kind of society it was intended for.

So to bring all this back to church, what I've done is treat the church as a design problem – take things apart, look at the pieces, see if they can be assembled in different ways, respond to emerging contexts, imagine alternative futures to aim for. It's playful in the sense of exploration without commitment to predetermined outcomes (which would prevent genuine break-throughs). This is very different from the Church's tendency to fix its forms for theological reasons. Churches often assume that they already have the right forms, having found out what God really wants. But I think God wants to play.

I'm also aware that spaces and objects shape our behaviour. They embody social arrangements and patterns of use that were current at the time, or were seen as a good thing. So, changing the spaces and objects changes what we can do, and what we think we can do. A stage divides people into actors and audience. A table for two is a different social situation from a table for 20. A beanbag implies a different set of behaviours (clothes, theologies) compared to a bench, and so on. Which is part of what instal-lation art is about.

> J: I like the sense that you pick up of saying to people, 'You can do it, too . . . it's really not that hard.' I feel like I am saying that to people all the time to try and demystify the whole thing. But it's still a big leap, people feel, to dive in. Alternative worship and its approach is still a marginal pursuit. Perhaps it's just such a different way of making a world?
>
> You've painstakingly documented alternative worship through photography. This has become an incredible archive/record/gift. <www.smallfire.org> is in some sense helping people remember and also sparking the imagination for ideas. Over the years you must have been to literally hundreds of worship experiences, installations, events, services. Are there a few memories that stick in your mind? Could you describe one or two and reflect on why they have struck you?

S: I think that people feel disempowered by things that appear to be big and complex, like church. People don't feel expert enough to tackle the 'professionals', especially in a field that stresses the virtue of obedience – and in any case we can't find the time – unless we start to think of the making of church as central to our lives and not just one more thing to be fitted in. Maybe it's like the difference between medicine – something you get from the experts – and health – something you look after yourself.

As you know, I started taking photographs of services to capture some of the beauty that was being discarded after an hour or so of existence. I couldn't convey to people what we were up to, without pictures. The words made no sense, until they had pictures to knock out the other church pictures they had in their heads. From architecture and punk, I know how important it is to record a movement for posterity! But I still wasn't prepared for what happened when I put the photo album on the internet. The emails that started to arrive, from Wisconsin or Wollongong, saying, 'How do we do this too . . . ?' ('You can do it, too . . . it's really not that hard').

As for memorable events: it's obligatory to mention Vaux's 'God is found in the shit' service, but I still think it was the best piece of boundary breaking I have experienced, in terms of behaviour and content. The shock value of breaking certain ecclesiastical taboos, the frisson of things that are 'profane', and yet a powerful and deeply moving act of worship precisely because it brought the 'dirt' into the church and told some uncomfortable truths. I wrote an article for Ship of Fools that concentrated on the outrageous images and acts, but in the centre of it all was a superb piece of contemporary dance using the whole length of the church, enacting Christ's journey to the cross with almost unbearable tension. I didn't even mention this – I rather regret that now. I also wish I had more and better photos, but I couldn't do it without breaking the electrifying atmosphere.

The Labyrinth in St Paul's Cathedral was obviously a major event with long-lasting ramifications, but the thing I want to pick out is the experience of lying on the floor looking up into the dome, in a state of relaxation while the crowds milled around. The Labyrinth allowed me to use St Paul's in a very different way, as a living room or leisure space almost, to take possession of it and be comfortable, to gaze and think without hurry. I had a similar experience later when the Labyrinth was in King's College chapel, Cambridge (and there was a heated floor there, too!). These experiences fed into my writings about churches used as chill-out spaces. It's such a different way of interacting with a church building. We usually stand around whispering, unsure of our rights, or we sit upright in uncomfortable chairs, to be schooled. In neither case can we experience church as a home, as a place in which we belong and which belongs to us and where we can pass the time. I think that there should always be floor cushions and sofas under the dome of St Paul's. It would say something very different about the house of God.

In a little bit of contrast to these dramatic events, I still remember Grace's 'homecoming' service from 1999. This was built around Henri Nouwen's book about Rembrandt's painting *The Return of the Prodigal*. It was classic 'old-skool' alt worship – stations made with slides and candles, each concentrating on one symbolic detail of the painting, in a huge dark church. Meditation, great art, quietness. I have only two photos to show how lovely it was. The station that I made was about 'true north'. It had a compass and magnets on a map, which ended up as one of the St Paul's Labyrinth stations. It was the original small ritual, the reason for the compass logo on <www.smallritual.org>.

J: In some of your reflections on <www.smallritual.org> you come up with some wonderfully playful rearrangements or redesigns of worship spaces both in church and in the culture. In church I am thinking, for example, of your idea of worship around a table with the pieces needed on it, or of pods, or the one where it is impossible to meet in a big group – that's a very subversive piece! And in the city the ideas of spirituality broadcast at points to your mobile phone or networks where the pieces of church/spirituality are scattered around the city. You are very imaginative. How do you come up with these ideas? The process for creating worship services and installations is a group effort but these are much more solo. How do you flex that creativity muscle, keep yourself fresh in imagining? A lot of these are provocations on a website. Do you have plans to realize any of them? I'd particularly love to see some of the ones in the city spaces.

S: A lot of my ideas are simply translations or applications from other fields into the field of church. For instance, the big tables have been done a few times in office fit-outs, for firms where people work on laptops and in fluid teams and don't need their own desks. And there are bench systems for desking where the individual work stations are replaced by one long worktop with legs only at the ends – this allows variable numbers of workspaces without changing the furniture. I often have lunch in a café with long communal tables – this is like the refectory of a monastery, so there's an easy link. Throw on the table the kind of stuff we routinely put on tables for stations at Grace, and there you have it.

In a similar way, the broadcast and network stuff is a reapplication of ideas about ubiquitous computing that have been around for years – in fact some aspects go back to 1960s' architectural theory. And a lot is just drawn from my everyday life and work in London, and wondering how spiritual expression can find a place in that.

What's radical, I suppose, is that I've applied these ideas to church. We seem to have got into a position where church buildings and rituals are disconnected from the general flow of cultural and technological change. Nobody thinks it subversive to explore how ubiquitous computing affects shopping or work or sport or art. But spirituality is assumed to be ancient and immutable, something removed from the rest of life, in opposition to technology and newness. Historical wisdom and a critique of society are good things, but Christianity as heritage or escape will be the death of it. It's not meant to be like that.

Two of the principles of alternative worship (or whatever you want to call it) are (1) your whole life is church and not just one event, and (2) apply all of your abilities to faith expression and don't accept compartments and boundaries. I am an architect specializing in corporate interiors. My work is about reinventing workplaces for organizations that are changing, usually in the direction of less hierarchy, greater fluidity, more openness. It's about the relationship between people, spaces, behaviour and technology. So I apply my knowledge to the church as if it were just another organization or workplace that needs to move forward.

Secular organizations spend a lot of time and money on this, because they believe that it makes them more productive and attractive to staff and customers. If churches were to spend comparably we might see some remarkable results. As it is, they seem to be locked into a narrow idea of what they are and do. A lot of that is about maintaining the glorious past rather than creating the vital future. There have been some wonderful new church buildings in the last 10 or 15 years. But I'm always disappointed by the same old schoolroom layout inside, as if what actually happens in the building could never change. I have myself been involved in actual church-building projects, once or twice, and I'm always itching to challenge their organizational and liturgical structure as part of the process (rather as Norman Foster reinvented his client's manufacturing process), but that's outside my remit when all they want is the font moving, which has taken five years to get agreement on. So I put out 'paper projects'. At least the ideas are out there, if anyone wants to pick them up. This is a noble and not entirely futile architectural tradition!

J: You have talked about the events or spaces and treating worship/church as a design problem. The tendency when people think about alternative worship is to look at the public event, the visible part. You edit the website <www. alternativeworship.org> and I know over the years you have handled many enquiries and questions from groups wanting to be part of the directory. As I understand it you have to say 'no' to some, not necessarily for stylistic reasons but more for reasons around values or process. Could you reflect on that? I think it connects with curation as that is also about process. What is important about the values and process of what has been called alternative worship? Is curation a logical extension of those values?

S: When groups apply to be on <www.alternativeworship.org> I go nosing around, as best I can, to get a feel for their organizational structure and values, because those are the things that determine whether you're alt worship or not. Surface style is helpful – style reveals where your head is at – so I like to see photos of events and people.

But what I'm looking at isn't style per se, but values communicated in other ways than words. You may have the candles and projectors, but who is in charge and where do they stand, and for how long? How many people make the events, and what (if anything) are those people called?

And because alt worship isn't defined by one style, feel/instinct comes into it a lot. Often one knows that something/someone is part of the movement, even though all the indicators are, on the surface, wrong. And sometimes something that seems the very essence of alternative worship is not – something in there is not quite right. Maybe the unspoken values or modus operandi are at odds with the declared intentions. Maybe it's all a marketing strategy.

But remember this is about inclusion in a website mapping a specific phenomenon, and not a final judgement on the worth of the church or person. They may be greater than us in the kingdom of heaven, but just not alternative worship. And this is a diverse movement, and people are on journeys, so I prefer to be inclusive.

For me the key attributes of alternative worship are a flat hierarchy and high levels of freedom and trust given to all individuals, so that what happens represents a cross-section of the community, not just one or two people. Or it represents one or two people, but a different one or two each time! What matters is not that everybody is involved, but that anybody can be who wants to be – and that everyone is encouraged to get involved somehow. So the first job of the curator is to open up a space where anyone can contribute on an equal level. This isn't about leadership so much as guardianship – the forum needs protection against those who would dominate it or misuse the freedom. You might say that the 'new' form of leadership is partly about preventing certain aspects of the 'old' form of leadership.

But the word 'leadership' is misleading. Speaking of curation acknowledges that we need the organizational and directional functions of traditional leadership, but that they don't have to come from the same source every time. Different people bring different flavours to the task, and the community is richer for experiencing them all. God is complex, and we are too. So one or two angles and approaches are probably not enough.

Throughout Christian history there has been a struggle between hierarchical and egalitarian models of the kingdom. The monarchical model, which appears to reify the structure of the late Roman imperial court, has faced a recurrent challenge from a radical egalitarianism which says that, for humans at least, all are equal before God. In support of the latter view is God's biblical tendency to work through the least, through outsiders, to subvert the status quo, culminating, of course, with the unauthorized rabbi Jesus and his socially dubious followers. Things are hidden from the wise and learned, and revealed to little children. So for me, the low-hierarchy open forum of alternative worship is about reconnecting to that biblical tradition, that God might work through anyone and we had better listen up. And after all, I'm one of the beneficiaries of that approach.

J: Some of the art/worship produced out of small collectives that function on the egalitarian model you describe has been wonderful. Yet it's always remained quite small or on the sidelines. Does that matter? Or has it had a wider renewing effect in the overall life of the Church? I wonder if egalitarian models are smaller because many people want just to come and consume rather than participate.

S: Small groups get stuff done. Most movements that change anything, whether in politics or the arts, are small groups with a common commitment to a cause or viewpoint. Small groups don't have passengers. I dare say that some of the dynamism of the early Church was about being small groups.

The other issue is about creating change. Groups working for change or the new are inevitably small because most of us, most of the time, rest content with the status quo. The status quo has formed us, which is why new ideas often seem 'cranky' to begin with (and the vested interests will do their best to make them seem so). It takes a minority prepared to be considered 'cranky' or subversive for long enough to spark wider change – the new has to be normalized somehow in people's minds. It has to become a genuinely possible alternative for people who are not pioneers, and that takes persistence.

I'm quite certain that people want just to come and consume. I often feel like that myself. As we've seen at Grace, the participatory model is better if you can take periods of rest now and then while others take the strain, which of course is harder in small groups, so it's a kind of vicious circle.

However, we need to see 'worship' – our gift and service to God – as more than just turning up and offering token participation in something set up by others. We've inherited a long tradition of passivity where things are done to and for us by 'experts'. It's a leap to become responsible for the forms of our spiritual lives. I hope alternative worship is an exploration of how we can do this together, as communities – because we need to do something bigger than ourselves.

> J: Of all the people I know, you probably have the best over-view of the movement, with your recording of what has happened. Of all the experimentation, theological takes, con-versations, networks, creative worship and installations, what will last? What's the legacy?

S: As for the second question, 'legacy' implies something that is over, and I'm hoping that we have a way to run with this thing yet! After 20 years I feel that we are only just beginning to make a real impact beyond the occasional minor sensation. We need to persist – persistence wins respect, because it shows that something has enduring value, can be developed, appeals to more than one audience.

I find it easier to think in terms of what has been demon-strated. One thing we have demonstrated is that a church service can take very diverse forms. People who want to do something different aren't stuck for models any more. Another thing demon-strated is that a community can generate its own faith expressions, and in a participatory way – valid and inspiring faith expressions are not the preserve of the professional clergy and 'experts'. I hope we've demonstrated a different role for the professionals and experts themselves, in supporting their faith communities.

One thing that will definitely last (because it's a function of the age we live in) is the ability of the laity to organize, debate and publish independently of the institutions. This is an effect of the internet rather than alternative worship, but alternative worship got in early and has shown various aspects of how such independent activity might look. We've shown how the functions of the institution, such as leadership, support and theological exploration, can happen through informal networks and personal initiatives rather than command-and-control structures – and that the results are not 'falling away' or heresy (the great fear that sustains the structures).

Of course, what I fear is that the legacy will be a makeover of the existing institutions that offers a bit more participation and sensory pleasure while leaving the power structures intact. I hope that church will always escape codification and control. I hope that the memory of alternative worship, like punk, is that you can always do something for yourself, if the thing that's being done for you isn't working.

The rise of the artist-curator

LAURA DRANE

Jonny: Laura, in your job you work with curators and groups putting on art events and exhibitions. As I understand it, in the art world curation is a relatively new idea and discipline. Can you give a few examples of how you have seen curation work really well? And if you had to tease it out, what exactly is it that a curator is trying to do?

Laura: My work generally involves project managing and consultancy in the arts and culture – in communities, through learning, with and for theatre companies, music organizations, galleries, and so on. Within that, I sometimes act as a curator, and sometimes work with other people's curation.

Curator literally means 'keeper' or 'carer', and is often used as a specific museums and galleries term, as the person who keeps or cares for a collection. You mention it came to the fore in recent times, but I think there's a long history of curation in the arts – just not as we now know it. There were at the very least dedicated collectors, keepers and carers from the Renaissance onwards and probably long before that as well – the Egyptians, Romans? The key to this change you're alluding to is the meaning of the language, specifically regarding the word 'curator'. It used to mean 'keeper' as in someone who collects, maintains, preserves, displays, cares for, but now it at least as much means 'interpreter' or 'programmer' as any of those things.

From my working and professional perspective, curation could be done by an individual or a group; by a professional or a volunteer; through pre-existing collections or objects, or through specifically commissioned new creations; in a specific spatial setting such as a gallery, or through something temporal like a festival.

In my working world and many other parallel ones, you can be seen to curate anything – it's as much of a job title that indicates a head of department as anything. For instance, I know someone who has a job title as 'Curator of Families'! The curation is the bringing together of the creative content within the practical aspects of the space, time-frame and budget. Again, it's messy – some curators would do all of these tasks, some wouldn't.

There are lots of recognized parallels with curation as well. In other spheres, curators might be known as programmers, editors, producers, even directors. There's a fascinating recent development on the emerging use of 'curation' to describe aggregation and editing in the media, with new technologies and on the web.

There are no hard and fast models, and some curators are territorial and precious. I once intimated that a collection piece from a museum might make sense in a show as part of a science festival and the collection's 'engineering curator' went berserk! Labels and language (as elsewhere in life) are very important.

You picked up on three considerations in the role of curation – imagination, articulation and continuity. They're certainly good ones to start with. The main issues I'd say are about control – of the story, of the selection, of the message(s), as a result of the curation.

Coming right down to it, this for me is the core question – is curation simply about arranging pieces neatly and presentably in an order in a space, or about telling a story, sending a message, taking the viewer/participant on a journey? Some of my most moving and meaningful worship experiences have been when the curator really acts as the curator, no more – pulling together the framework for worship, the order in and of the space, and allows others to bring and interpret the content without control. But I'd say it's far from the norm to be that open and collaborative.

You ask for some examples of good curation. Maybe it's easier to say what bad curation does! It jars the flow of information and exploration; it simply collects and assembles a set of pieces/objects. Good curation orders, gives meaning and message, references, questions/queries. The best is almost invisible, however heavy the subtext.

I wonder if some of the best examples I've seen as a punter are ones that allow you to make your own story from experiences, your own narrative – and they are usually ones that are curated for those for whom this sort of discussion is entirely remote (children, and people who wouldn't normally attend). The touring Miffy exhibition was simply delightful and, despite wanting to hate it, the V&A touring Kylie show was likewise. Another example is when the Meltdown festival is 'guest directed' – I often think the term curated might be better applied. Almost all of those are stunning, whether you think you'd like the content or not.

For me, it comes down to the best curation being about identifying, selecting, sorting, (de/re)constructing, labelling, storytelling, transposing. It can be viewed as production, programming, and spatial/temporal display.

The fascination for me in being involved in this debate is that it's like having a true outsider (with all due respect!) look in on what is not normally a public facet of this work. This conversation is pulling the term and its use in one sphere into another one – it's liberating, messy and blurred, but good! Curators are like anthropologists or ethnologist/ethnographers – they broker and present a view of the world and a message to others outside that view. And we only need anthropologists or ethnologist/ethnographers to explain us to others, not to ourselves.

J: You have described curation in a number of contexts. One of the major types of spaces to curate in is a gallery or museum. I have found it fascinating reading how different curators see themselves and their role in relation to institutions, and also how the institutions' view of themselves seems to have shifted over time. At one extreme you have the view that the museum is the power broker, with the money and control, subservient to the social interests of the day, static and unmoving, detached from life and the public. The day you take a job as a curator in the institution your artistic vision is over, you've sold out! On the other hand, other curators have managed to work with, in and for museums and galleries and negotiate between artists and the institution to create some amazing things. Johannes Cladders talked about the museum as a space of risk,[1] which I love. Thinking about the museums in London, some are very experimental. But I suspect that if you rewound, things used to be a lot more stuffy. How do you see this interplay of artists, curators and the negotiation of newness in institutional life in the art world? And where should a curator seek to locate within that?

I can see a similar set of negotiations around the church and worship – innovation at the edges, space in institutions in some places, and everything in between, but we also badly need newness. I have tended to favour both – that is, if you get people working at the centre and at the edge you are likely to see some change. But I don't hear of many cathedrals or churches seeing themselves as a space of risk!

L: As you simply describe the scenario/landscape, power and control has moved from institutions to individuals. I'd say this is broadly true, though I think you have to see the biggest picture in all of this too – in 1970, the whole world was changing, not just art and galleries. So, of course, everything is subject to the influence of the whole and external factors, not just internal debates and forces and players. I really don't think you can under-play the significance of that – we're all postmodern now . . .

To specifically address your question, though, I'd say that change in this way (the interplay around newness) could be seen, not just in freelance and maverick curators given 'permission to play nicely' in the institutions (or not), but also in the appearance and rise of the artist-curator.

Some parallel context: I was having a conversation with a colleague earlier in the week about 'talent', specifically in music – we settled on interest, capacity, technical proficiency/skill, creative thinking, among other things. Within this, we finally came round to the potentially offensive idea that musicians in the Western classical movement, however good or talented, would be considered to be 'interpreters' of their art, and subject to the 'originator' powers of both the composer and the conductor. And we wondered if any potentially significant shift in that genre is much more likely to come from the originators (composers in particular) than the interpreters (players). However, the ultimate originator-interpreter option could lie with a composer-player, if there is such a thing: they would have the idea (originate) and write a piece (interpret), then set/conduct (originate) and perform it (interpret). I suppose in another genre – popular music – you could say that was what really good bands do . . .

So we concluded that unless you can subvert or challenge or throw away the rules on both origination and interpretation (creation and execution), you can't create a significant shift in a genre or field, however good or talented you might be. Going back to bands, think about the making and presentation of popular music before punk. Now think of the Sex Pistols or Joy Division. Before them, it was accepted that you needed a certain musical proficiency (interpretation) and song-writing skills (origination) to make popular music. The likes of Joy Division decided that playing instruments 'properly' was a luxury they could take or leave; thus they originated and interpreted not just their songs, but their whole style and approach, therefore changing and challenging the wider genre of popular music too. My colleague's other example was U2, saying that they were a rubbish band when they started out because they couldn't play like everyone else; they made their own style, played like no one else, and maybe that's a key to why they were distinctive enough to have longevity of success.

So, creating a significant shift or exploding a genre takes someone to say, 'It doesn't have to be done like that.' Maybe they

don't intend to also say, '. . . in fact it *has* to be done differently';
maybe they just don't know any better; maybe they are rebelling
against the norm; maybe it's a more positive form of creative
disruption.

Let's make a parallel leap from music to the visual arts, still
thinking about origination and interpretation. Unlike players of
Western classical music, visual artists are both their own originators (creators of an idea) and interpreters (execution). (Leave to
one side the likes of Damien Hirst who have teams of fabricators
who make their work for them.) Individual artists can create
a revolution in their own art practice by pushing to the limits
the creation and execution of their own work. This would mean
that they wouldn't just be creating new pieces, but new formats/
styles – say, like the development of installations or site specifics
as art, or live art performances/events as art.

But however influential that may turn out to be, that's only one
artist's practice, not the curation of their work with and alongside
others, or considering its influence on the wider structures such
as galleries and museums. So can we also add another dimension
here – the curator, as the person who gives context and subtext to
a set of displayed pieces, bringing their origination (commissioning/
gathering/collection) and interpretation (display) into play.

Add all of that together in one person and see what happens.
When the artist, already their own originator-interpreter of their
piece/work, also acts as their own curator, they can explode the
genre/field. And so the arrival of the artist-curators surely signalled
that a change was going to come. Think Warhol and The Factory.
Think the Young British Artists curating their own postgrad shows
in dilapidated warehouses in London's East End. That's your revolution in newness, I would say. Some did it from rebellion against
the institutions, some from ignorance of the expected norms, some
from a genuinely creative disruption. But change came as a result.

I'm not sure I can make a third parallel leap into church/
worship after all that! Maybe you can reflect that back to me, if
you can see it in there somewhere . . .

I do think there's lots to say about control generally, as you point out.

- Curatorial control of both the message and the medium.
- Control of the structures and of the creative content (what's allowed, by whom, and so on).
- Control of the story of the pieces, and their selection, presentation, interpretation and display.
- Control of interplays between the creator, the interpreter and the viewer/participant.

Control has been addressed a lot lately when rethinking issues around the narrative of collections or pieces. For instance, an artefact from a warship might not just be the story of that time, those travels and victories, but also of the person that made it or used it, and of the 'losing side' too in some cases. This has happened particularly when addressing racial or ethnic diversity; a recent example might be the reinterpretation of items linked to the slave trade.

> J: I like the way you describe the artist-curator – fantastic. No need to make the leap into church – I think it's there for all to see. Alternative worship is full of artist-curators. A few people in conversation have been trying to weigh up if they are artist or curator but you have given a way to describe it as both – you have described me at least.
>
> Have you talked yourself into saying something about control? You've used the word so many times, and mentioned Joy Division! I like the headings you have laid out on it. In relation to church it immediately lays out why this approach is so powerful and subversive and why trust is such a key issue for artist-curators of worship – trust between public, artists, institution, curator. The flip side of it is permission, of course.

L: At work, I'd never say I was an artist-curator – I might be a curator, or would say I am a producer, or director, or project manager. But at Sanctus1 I'd say I am very definitely an artist-curator. 'Artist' is such a loaded term in my professional sphere. So much so, that many people preface it – they are 'practising artists', or 'community artists'. And if we wandered not too much further down that route then eventually we'd bump into the professional/amateur debate.

Rereading what I've written, I'd just want to restate even more clearly that if artists are their own originator-interpreters, then of course curators can also be their own originator-interpreters (without having to be artist-curators). A curator originates (creates) the collection of pieces around a theme and its subtext, and interprets (executes) it in terms of their more pragmatic installation, display, labelling. Both have power and influence and reach in their own ways, with peers/colleagues and within the broader sector. But the merger of the two in one person – the artist-curator – is the potential explosion or significant shift. That is what I am trying to get at.

OK, control: here we go . . .

It's still the elephant in the room to some extent, in terms of my professional sphere, and I'd say in church/worship too. We all know it's an issue, but who's going to really address it, and how? I wasn't joking that much when I said that some curators have been given 'permission to play nicely' in the institutions (or not). However we relate to them, the institutions are still just that and hold a lot of power and control – about what is allowed, and by whom. So they have given permission to, and even embraced, some of these mavericks, but some institutions have very definitely held it all at arm's length or pushed it as far away as possible.

Using the previous language, curators are their own originator-interpreters: they originate (pull together or commission) a collection of pieces around a theme and create the subtext, and they interpret it in terms of their concerns around installation, display, ordering. This gives them control of the content and the style, of what to show and how – of the message and the medium, if you like. At its best, it's a powerful and transformative process for curator, artist and viewer. My aside to that would be that the best curators are always going to take you on a journey, even if you don't know it as the viewer, or agree with it as the artist.

Control of the selection, interpretation and presentation of pieces also bumps up against the idea that there is no one right way to approach curation and, of course, no one response. Each piece or collection of pieces necessarily reflects back the context of an individual's opinion, story, experience – whether that is of the person who created or made it, or curated it, or is viewing it. What are its history and references? How is it seen, what does it say? What response does it invoke? So combine a maker's or an artist's individual reflected context with a curator's, and then again with a viewer's, and you can start to see how layered and complex a process it can be.

Artists might make a piece; and either they let it be what it is and you make of it what you will; or they might have ideas they want to underline about its meaning, subtext and references. Curators interpret their own response to that piece and place it in relationship with others. Then viewers bring their own interpretation as well. It can get very layered very quickly. Again, we're all postmodern now.

Institutionally, curators also tend to be heads of departments and seen as experts, giving them influence and status in their organizations and the sector. Even as freelancers/independents, they are significant figures because they are the creative and driving force, they *make shows happen*. This can give them a measure of control of and within the structures (the buildings, the funding streams), in addition to their creative control.

Rethinking issues around the narrative of collections or pieces has been the big one in the last few years – even down to why some pieces have survived and were collected over others, never mind the stories they reflect or tell.

You mention trust. That's exactly the issue, for me anyway. And if the flip side is permission: some will seek it and wait for it; some will just do it anyway; some won't know they were supposed to even ask for it or have it bestowed.

J: So what? How does all this experience in curation and the art world affect your approach and set of instincts when it comes to creating worship in Sanctus1?

L: Before getting into curating worship in Sanctus1 . . . I think if we're not careful we can read into this conversation so far that we're only talking about new/contemporary visual artists. In your reflection on curating beyond the canon, there was a quote about artists who have worked in cultural space changing ambitions when they work for an institution. The example given was that all of a sudden they want to do a Warhol exhibition, which was described as being pretty lame, a sell-out. Sure – to decide to curate a Warhol exhibition just because he's well known might signal the end of a creative career and someone buying into the institutions. But to curate it at a point and time and place in the broader culture where Warhol's work would challenge the status quo (hard to imagine maybe, since it's now so tame and ubiquitous) would be a truly brave statement.

Think also about how older work might have historical and contemporary relevance/resonance. For instance, programming the Greek tragedy *Antigone* at the Royal Exchange Theatre in 2008 brought almost 2,000 years of history bang up to date – about women's social status and empowerment, about just and unjust war . . .

The point is that what is chosen to be curated can be a carefully crafted statement to and of culture.

OK, so in relation to Sanctus1, you asked 'So what?' Great question! Obviously, the right answer is that my working life has nothing whatsoever to do with church – doesn't everyone else just leave their personalities, skills and experiences at the door on the way in? (Only kidding!)

I'd preface this entire section with the words 'for me'. The stuff that follows is how I think I operate in Sanctus1, but other people who co-curate or add content alongside me might disagree, and I know others who take a wholly different approach to curating worship in and of and for the community.

I would say that my preference is to work as an artist-curator at Sanctus1 – both masterminding the framework for worship and, alongside others, contributing to the content. My approach would be to try to create spaces for and with people to explore a theme, in both planning and engaging with worship.

Generally, I'd aim to be both as consensual and as dictatorial as possible! I like to get input, ideas and content from other people, places, and so on, while creatively driving the vision and often contributing content myself.

I'd say that there's some value in going back to Sheikh's schema for the future of curation containing the three elements – articulation, imagination and continuity. To use his language: I'd aim to articulate a theme, an idea, a set of questions or responses, a theology; I'd aim to use an imaginative, holistic and multi-sensory approach to engage every part of us as people; and I'd aim to root that in the continuity of culture, other S1 services, The Church, and so on.

I'd almost always start with an idea for a theme or something that's inspired me or I want to explore – essentially, what message/subtext to curate. It's usually something from culture that I think speaks into church and worship and/or back to the wider culture. From experience, it could be almost anything – an advert, a novel, a film, a band/track/album, a TV show. Sometimes it's a question: what did Jesus do with his last hours on earth (inspired by Mark Owen's song 'Four Minute Warning'), or do we really know how to thirst or hunger (inspired by sitting in a sauna!)? As you can see, we 'magpie' a lot!

Once that's decided, context is all: it's the space, the ethos, the atmosphere, the setting, the timing, the motivation. Planning a wedding or baptism is very different from planning worship for a Sanctus1 evening, for instance. I'd then start to think about the pragmatics – put simply, the who, what, when, where, why and how. That would start to define my own initial approach to planning.

Working from a theme/idea and context, then, I'd usually gather anything from one to half a dozen other people around the theme. Very, very occasionally I'd plan and execute a service by myself, but I find it less fulfilling, less challenging, less creative – though sometimes it's just quicker and easier to get on and do it yourself! So we'd meet and kick ideas around, come up with responses and questions and avenues to explore. Then normally – and this is the curator bit – I'd prefer to creatively frame and drive it from that point on, then delegate back out different elements within the framework – activities, set up, liturgy, roles/functions – to those who want to contribute. Sanctus1 services that I lead on might be artist-curated by me, but the best ones are truly 'group shows'.

However, many of the most spiritually moving and engaging services I've had the privilege to curate would be ones that I've not had my own 'work' in – what I might call 'straight curation'. We sometimes create and do services from scratch on the afternoon or evening we meet within Sanctus1 and those for me tend to push the most boundaries. You never know what anyone's going to do or bring; you have no or little control; the curation might be the fixed framework but the content is always surprising. Truly more than the sum of its parts, maybe this approach also leaves even more space for God to break in. We've done this quite frequently in Sanctus2nds (our intergenerational service) and also on our meeting on Wednesday nights.

Cheryl Lawrie and I had a conversation recently about the process of planning worship versus the 'turning up and engaging with it'. She says it so much better than I could:

> I know that the people who talk to me about curating get far more energy back from the process than what they think they put into it. If you work with a team of people that you love; if you're not doing it every week or even every month;

if this is how you work out what you believe and who you are; if, as someone recently said to me, life makes more sense when you're doing this; then it's time well spent . . . and if not, there are plenty of other ways to plan worship . . .

The sense is that the richness is in the creating, planning, curating, and that it almost feels as if those participating on the day are getting a diminished experience by not having been involved in the process; they're getting the best 'remnants' of the process, as Cheryl and I call them, but they're still only the bits that are left to show.

I've just been pondering the nuanced difference of language between promoting something as a repeated or one-off single thing, such as a gig or theatre performance, and curating something, which is more a set of things pulled together, like an exhibition or festival. It says something to me about the difference between just doing a service (using a fixed/set liturgy, say) and making a worship event, and something about how collaborative a worship event is. If curation is about bringing together a set of things to relate, juxtapose, inform, reference, then I think in worship it's even more about bringing together a set of people to do that.

Here's a quote that I love, attributed to Willem Sandberg, director of the Stedelijk Museum, Amsterdam and organizer of the first CoBrA exhibition in 1949:

> After war
> I asked myself
> what arts reply would be
> to all these huge changes
> in human relationships
> The famous artists hardly responded
> I was about to turn away
> when I noticed a group of young people
> who had something to say
> and who said it on a new note violently

in a primitive way perhaps
They were seeking a new language
with much warmth and resolution.

J: I agree about the Warhol thing. Part of the reason the idea appeals to me, I think, is that I am a bit more interested in the edge and newness than just curating a famous artist for its own sake. I also like provocative things that may overstate something but get a reaction. Of course, doing a show of an artist does have intrinsic value in and of itself. I recently went to a Warhol show at the Hayward Gallery and enjoyed it, especially the way it was curated. Though I did enjoy even more the show with a younger lesser-known artist upstairs.

I wanted to reflect on where you see God in relation to all this? You said, 'Maybe this approach also leaves even more space for God to break in.' I was intrigued by that phrase. Art is full of moments, of experiences, of epiphanies. And equally I can think of those moments in worship. Can you perhaps pick one or two moments where you have sensed this 'breaking in', as you put it? And can you reflect on how the Spirit of God might be at work in that?

L: I think when I'm artist-curating worship the chances are that I've planned and done everything to the nth degree, so much so that I can't really participate in the worship. And I feel that that tends to allow less space for God somehow (maybe that's just for me, rather than for the participants/worshippers). So what do I think it looks and sounds and feels like when God breaks in? These are a couple of examples from 'straight curation' events.

At Sanctus2nds, we made microwave bread for use during communion, and Andy took it up to the table to break during the liturgy/prayer and this huge plume of steam rose up out the bread. You could not have planned it – the beauty, the simplicity, the symbolism!

In 2nds again, we usually have a café space and there's often dried fruit and biscuits for everyone to munch on. We normally do communion in small groups around the café table, and when everyone was sharing the bread, Jude (my then two-year-old godson) offered me half of his half-eaten dried mango slice. See, he got it and interacted.

One other time in Sanctus, we used Si Smith's 40 slides, set to Snow Patrol's 'Run'. It sounds mildly ridiculous on paper, but it was way more than the sum of its parts in that service.

These examples remind me that the best curated spaces should leave room for interaction and response, not just of and from the participant/viewer/worshipper, but also of and from God.

Is the Spirit a co-curator, a co-artist, in our creation and execution – does she gift us ideas and synergy? Is the Trinity the ultimate Artist-Curator? I root myself and my worship curation in the knowledge that because God is the ultimate creator, then everything we do imperfectly but sincerely reflects that ultimate creative act and its originator.

Stumbling into something lovely

CHERYL LAWRIE

—————•◦•—————

Jonny: One of the things I have found really interesting and hopeful in the last few years is that a lot of alternative worship groups are choosing to create art/worship experiences/installations/journeys in public spaces such as art galleries, city centres, beaches or parks. Nic Hughes proposed a toast in a comment on my blog to what he termed 'the new itinerants, the new walkers, the new turn in the organism formerly known as alt worship' – that is, seeing it wandering in public spaces. You have curated worship in a city centre car park, which is such a great idea but how did that come about? Why that space? And can you describe maybe one of the installations/happenings you have done in there?

Cheryl: There were a couple of things that started us looking for a public space – I'd been wondering for quite a while about what would happen to the content of worship/sacred space if we changed the context and took it seriously, and I wanted to see what happened to our theology and expressions of spirituality when they had to make sense in (and of) a public space. And then a friend who isn't part of the church arrived really late to a space that we were curating in a city church, and she told me that she had walked around the block for 30 minutes before she had plucked up the courage to come inside. I felt sick that we'd made something so hard for her to come to.

So I looked for a space for a while but nothing felt quite right, or fell into place. I have no idea how the idea to use the car park came to me; it was just one of those ideas that came fully formed! I sent an email to the building manager with a 'You're going to think I'm mad' subject heading, and he replied an hour later, 'Yes you are, and yes you can,' and we were off.

The car park is in the basement of my office building in the centre of Melbourne. It's used during the week but is empty over weekends. It's a basic underground city car park with no frills – I've never measured it up, but it fits 18 cars with room to move, and it's big enough to need to use a lot of 20-metre extension leads. It's all concrete and open, with the exception of big pillars in the centre, and a passageway that leads to nowhere up one end. The ceiling is mostly a mass of pipes, which are coated in 30 years of grime (we're gradually cleaning them off as we go!). It's got its issues: there are only three power points in the whole basement, and when we're setting up we have to avoid the dripping pipes and ratsack. We have to clear out the junk that's accumulated down there each time, and then put it back where it was when we've finished. We normally have to wash down the entrance of the car park with bleach to get rid of the urine smell from the laneway outside, and clear up the glass from the previous night's broken bottles. (I was asked by the building manager to hire security guards for the first couple of spaces we curated, but they seem less anxious about that now.) We can only use the space on weekends – a Saturday space means that we bump in and out on the same day, which makes for 15 or 16 hours of solid work. The great thing is that there's nothing that can be broken, and there are very, very few restrictions on what we can do. It's a physically demanding space – we go home really dirty and with everything aching after curating a space – but it's absolutely fantastic to use.

When we curate spaces we generally open them up for a few hours for people to wander through. We call them art installations/ sacred spaces, but the language is really awkward, and we have to find better ways to communicate and advertise what we're actually doing. Normally they involve interactive art, music and multimedia – our intention is that people can participate, and that the space will be different because they have been there.

One example was a space we were asked to curate last year for a festival being held in Melbourne. We used the theme 'holy ground: holy city', drawing off the story of Moses and the burning bush, and the image of the holy city in Revelation. We wanted to explore the idea that if the holy city was the end point of creation, then proclamations of freedom and acts of redemption (the burning bushes of our time) should be happening around us now in the city.

The first thing you saw when entering was a projection onto the ceiling of a video that one of the team, Blythe, took of people walking through Melbourne's laneways through the lunchtime peak hour. In the centre of the basement we wrapped 'danger tape' around the four concrete pillars, making out a large empty rectangle, and we stuck 'No standing any time – holy ground' signs onto the pillars, the obvious implication being that God might be speaking through an ugly slab of concrete. (We hung some shoes from a pipe by the pillars, like the shoes you see hanging from powerlines – that idea was a last-minute moment of genius from someone on the team.) The other elements of the space were small – we figured that most acts of redemption are small, and that if we don't look we'll miss them, and we wanted the space to echo that. We projected different video loops taken around the city, but made the images very small and put them in dark spaces, or down near the floor (we project straight onto the concrete). We stuck photos of ordinary city places and moments onto the walls in obscure places and wrote around them, with reflections of what life is like in the city, and asking where the work of God might be happening (because of us and in spite of us). We hung iPods in custom-made frames and placed them around the car park (the frames were wrapped in danger tape too), showing movies of moments where redemption has happened in cities: monks marching in Rangoon the week before, protesting at the oppression of Burmese people; the famous video of the student standing before the tanks in Tiananmen Square; the collapse of the Berlin Wall. We used a slide projector right at the end of the passageway that goes to nowhere, projecting slides of people cross-ing a city intersection – probably half the people who came wouldn't have found the passageway, and some would have been put off by the rat poison, but those who walked up there would have seen a contextual version of the 'holy city' passage written on the concrete around the slide projector, which you could only read when the light came up – it was really lovely. There was a café in the space offered by another group, and we put some ques-tions and statements for reflection on those tables. We were aim-ing for a mixture of provocation, proclamation and prayer.[1]

This space was particularly multimedia-rich; normally there's more installation art. It was open for a few hours each day of the weekend. I have no idea how many people came through – quite a lot, by memory. I do remember that some people loved it and spent hours wandering through and talking about what they were thinking in response (I always think that a space has worked when people talk about what they're thinking because they've been there, rather than telling you how clever you've been); some people were completely underwhelmed and thought there was no point to it at all . . . Remembering that they could be right keeps us healthy, I think!

> J: How does the process work for you? You do some things on your own, I know, but in this context it was with a team. How does it work for a team pulling this together? When you are in an ideas phase, how do you sift what to go with and what to let go? I like it that some things just happen, like the shoes when you are setting up the space.

C: The stuff I do on my own always feels like a pale imitation of what we do as a team. I keep wanting to say, 'I don't know, we just do it and sometimes it works,' but that's not helpful to me or you.

This all sounds so deliberate. Half of what we do is a complete accident . . . that's not quite true, but random-ness and intuition have a really big part to play.

The team that puts together the basement spaces (which is more a collective than a community) is made up of people who responded to an invitation on my blog, and others who heard about what we were doing and then wanted to get involved. There are six regulars, and a few irregular add-ons. We meet once a month for a drink, between spaces, and much more frequently in the lead-up to a space (we do around four a year). We've gone about it all the wrong way, in a sense: no discernment process or community building or defined missional focus – all the things I would recommend! We just wanted to get in there and make spaces and play. I have thought that we exist purely to create spaces, but everyone in the group has their own reasons for coming: for some it's deconstructing years of institutionalized faith damage; for others it's connecting faith and imagination when that's not possible anywhere else; for another it's community. I guess the creating of spaces is the common way we work all that out. Probably half of our success is that we don't take ourselves or what we do too seriously, and that we do it for ourselves, really. I can't speak for the rest of the group, but I don't care whether what we do works for anyone else – I just love the process of imagining faith, rather than thinking about it.

The team is amazing, and we're so lucky with our skill base – but every group of people has amazing skills, we're nothing extraordinary. Perhaps the only skill that really matters is knowing what it's possible for us to do, and leaving the rest to everyone else.

I can never remember what process we use to get us started, and as such I panic each time. Mostly it involves a few drinks, food, throwing around concepts, trying to work out the feel we want to have, and agreeing again that we have to do better publicity this time. The spaces have always been tied to an event – Easter, Christmas, Valentine's Day, the solstices – which focuses us a little. We always start with ideas, and work a theology into the ideas that take hold (sort of a retrospective justification! – though I think theology matters a lot, and there has to be theological continuity in what we do; if we can't fit decent theology into an idea, then we ditch the idea). Our problem is much more likely to be too many ideas, but sometimes you can have pages of brilliant ideas and none of them is actually good for the space or context. I think we probably spend two meetings throwing ideas around without thinking that we have to make them work, or kidding ourselves that they are anything like how the finished product will be – brainstorming, but trying to add layers to ideas too.

The selection of ideas is tricky – it seems to be an intuitive process, not rational. My failing is that I wet-blanket things far too quickly, which is the worst possible thing to do. But we're getting good as a group now at being intuitive, and knowing what works. The best ideas are always the ones that aren't obvious, that have multiple layers, or take what we were originally wanting to say and twist it completely. It's nice when we're surprised by something.

I do the write-up after each meeting – we rarely make decisions about what's in or out at meetings (decision-making is not our collective gift!). I write up what I remember of what we talked about, and at that point ideas that are half-formed, that ran out of energy or that I can't make sense of get left off the list. When I send notes out I tell people that they're incomplete, and we can put discarded ideas back in; sometimes we do, sometimes we don't. It's very undemocratic on one level – which I find awkward, but people stand up for ideas when they really want to, and it seems to work.

I think that part of what makes a space work is being willing to throw out the best ideas because sometimes they're not the right ones, or to drop stuff that seemed pivotal in the beginning but no longer quite fits. We often get to a point in the process and ditch everything we've thought of to start again. Anything that tries to be clever normally ends up looking stupid and forced, so we try to avoid that . . . but we do leave in a lot of things that we don't quite get or understand ourselves – they're often the best parts of a space. I'd really love to hear how others do this sifting, because it all seems so random . . .

After a few meetings it kind of consolidates, or perhaps it's just that a looming event forces clarity. People take responsibility for different parts of the space. I check in with everyone, and make sure it's holding together, and write copious lists of what to do and what we need. A couple of us will normally do a full day sometime in the week before, pulling everything together, and on the day it's all hands on deck for making it work. We're perfectionists – it's so lovely working with a group that thinks the little tiny details matter.

> **J:** One theme I've been reading about that I like is articulation[2] – that in curating you are articulating something. It may be open to exploration but there is a narrative, a take, an idea. In the example you describe it's around redemption happening if we have eyes to see in city spaces. You are making/imagining a different city, a different world, both in the event and in the space you are in. I think this is a tricky thing to wrap your head round in two ways. The first is in the tone of the articulation – keeping it open and invitational and journeying together rather than being imposed. And second, that there is a world to make, an articulation. Part of the problem, it seems to me, is that so much of the Church and the world is numb – they have very little that catches the imagination, or at least that catches mine, in this rich way. Perhaps they are happy with the dominant consciousness?! Where do you discover the resources to re-imagine the world? How do you discover something that you want to articulate enough to put this level of creative energy into?

C: I so love this. I can't imagine a better description of what we'd like to do than re-imagine the world. So much of the worship in which I've participated in the past has tried to control the meaning (planning begins with the question, 'What's the message people need to hear?'), and never lets there be the possibility of an alternative interpretation to a story. So even if worship is creative, it's descriptive rather than evocative – it might use film clips, but it will use them to tell you what you should be thinking. I wonder if that's also what creates the blandness: when someone else does all the work for you, and doesn't make you enter into the story to make it your own; or when worship becomes the lowest common denominator of understanding and participation.

I don't know, though, that we start with the intention to re-imagine the world. I think our intention is to put our human stories against a larger story, and to let them shape each other, so we look for resources that tell the story or make the link, or make it safe for people who come to do that. We almost always make everything ourselves – I can't remember using other people's stuff, although we probably have (and we certainly have for inspiration, as ideas to bounce off). It's not that we don't like what others are doing, it's that part of the reason we're doing this is to make sense of stuff ourselves – the act of creating is half the point.

When I showed this to Blythe, an artist in our team, she suggested that a curator has a very selective role, deciding what a viewer's experience will be by selecting and interpreting an artist's work and placing it into a context. She said that maybe we're artists, not curators, and maybe that's why stuff seems more open ended . . .

This is probably overanalysing, but when we're thinking about words for a space it starts with simply stating a reality (this is how the world is), but then includes the underlying things beneath the reality (the questions or fears or existential angst that are common to all of us, that shape our presence in the world). I don't know whether everyone in the group would say that the Christian story is the answer for all our existential questions, but I think we're all pretty convinced that things like grace, love, hope, redemption, forgiveness and justice are worth investing in – that they make up part of a bigger story that we'd want to put our own stories alongside. That becomes the third layer, which I guess is the re-imagining you're talking about. That's probably the point where things could get declarative – perhaps what saves us is that we simply don't have that confidence in faith. Speaking only for myself, while I really want to believe that there's a grace beyond human making that transforms the broken and shattered, I can't declare it absolutely, but I'm willing to entertain it as a possibility. So the 'bigger story' becomes a question or provocation in the space. I think we've curated a good space when it's possible for people to let go of other stuff they're really sure of (grief, fear, desolation) and to risk the possibility of grace and see what happens. Sometimes I think we're daring God to show up. I also think it's irresponsible to invite people to re-imagine the world without acknowledging the hesitation/risk/cost/stupidity involved in them choosing that alternative, so in the back of my mind I want to honour those who decide it's just too hard.

The other thing we try to do is tell a story from as many different perspectives as possible (for example, hope as told by the idealist, the cynic, the saved, the betrayed, the desperate) and hopefully remember that there's a perspective that we haven't thought of yet, so letting another interpretation be possible, even if it hasn't been articulated.

And our bottom line, if we can't manage that, is that it has to be beautiful, and fun, and a little bit quirky.

I love that we don't have a vested interest in the outcome of what we do, which means that we can stop just before reaching a conclusion – we let the last bit of whatever go unsaid. People have to write their own ending, and do their own work.

I can't speak for the others, but the exhausting thing for me is the energy it takes to empathize – to find the words and create the space that might resonate with someone who's been betrayed by hope; that will honour their story and find where faith speaks into that . . . The rest of it is only energizing. When it stops being fun, I hope we'll just stop doing it.

> J: Several people have said that it is a chaotic/accidental approach that seemed to enable the creative stuff.

C: It's funny, so much of the process is accidental, but when it comes to putting the space on, we're control freaks. Partly that's because we're who we are, but it's also about responsibility: if our intention is to make spaces that will move people to re-imagine the world, then we're inviting them into a different headspace (beyond the rational) – and people won't move into that imaginative space if they're anxious about something falling off walls, or if things don't flow, or aren't clear, or if they're worried that we're going to manipulate them without their knowing. It doesn't mean that things have to be perfect, but it does mean not overreaching or doing stuff that we can't do, and our intention is to make things seamless. Stuff goes wrong, of course, but much less when we don't try too hard to be clever, and when we're really well prepared.

If we expect people to lose themselves in a space – which is a massive risk for people – first we've got to earn their trust and then respect it, and then we have to put as few barriers in their way as possible. I think I said this before, but we can tell when it's worked – people come out talking about how their world has changed, rather than how creative we are.

> J: I was interested in the comment about whether in creating worship we are artists or curators. The difference, I guess, is that most people curating worship are also producing something for it – though not always. It's quite different from getting to know a particular artist's work and working with them to exhibit it. That strand of the 'curator as creator' is definitely one approach in the art world and perhaps this is closer to what was being said?

C: I've been thinking about this. I think, in our planning, that most of the group 'act' as artists, and I 'act' as curator, at least in the beginning stages. I haven't asked them about that. We've been having an email conversation around the group over the last week about the solstice space. They keep coming up with the beautiful ideas; I'm the one who says, 'It'll look gorgeous – how can it add meaning to the space?'

I probably took that role in the beginning because this was my project, and my space, and I had overall responsibility for it, but at that point the group curating the spaces was changing each time, so we had to inculturate people into what we were doing. I think there's a far greater group ownership of the philosophy now; or, more realistically, the group has self-selected to only include those with that philosophy, and the curating responsibility is really shared much more.

I think I imagined right at the beginning that the basement spaces would have a particular purpose, and I held to that purpose rather than letting the various people who indicated interest dictate what the spaces would look like. I had a hunch that there were people who were looking for a space to explore the evocative (and the doubt/uncertainty/unfinishedness that the evocative evokes!). Those places are few and far between, and I knew that it would take a while for those people to emerge. If people simply wanted to explore imagination and art in worship, then I hoped that there would be other places they could do that (and certainly within the Uniting Church here there's plenty of space for that). So the idea or philosophy formed first, and then the group of people formed around it.

> **J:** You have used the word evocative to describe the tone of what you present and what you respond to. I like the contrast you make with being descriptive. This is the crux of good articulation, I suspect. You do have a vision, a world to make, but it's offered as a question, tentatively or humbly and in hope. And it's probably a question you are still asking rather than something that is resolved. There's a growing boredom I have noticed in evangelical and charismatic churches in the UK, particularly around worship, and it's being discussed in articles and online. Some of the symbolic responses and ritual and art and liturgy that are familiar to those of us who have been part of the alternative worship movement is being drawn upon. But it often is certain or descriptive or sewn-up. I hope this is just because it's young in those traditions.

C: I've seen people take core ideas that we've used, and add their own interpretation over the top to make it fit a theology they want to communicate – which is (I keep telling myself) fine. Of course, I do the same in reverse – we take the stuff of culture, the Bible and tradition, and add an alternative meaning to it. How on earth can I deny someone else the right to do that? But it's weird, watching stuff being appropriated in ways that are different from how I imagined. When I think people are missing the point to it all, I try to remember that they may have a different point that's just as valid.

And, if I think about it, I am where I am now because of the certainty I've had in the past. When I look back at the stuff I did a few years ago, when I was first exploring alt worship, it was much more descriptive (I came from a liberal/progressive tradition – we were just descriptive about the inclusive, social justice aspects of every story). But I don't know that you can do this for long without being changed by the process of creating: the inevitable ambiguity of music and art that doesn't rely on words; the invitational and participatory nature of alt worship (participation meaning that people influence the outcome) that means that people will bring their minds to stuff, which changes both them and us. I think alternative worship in conservative settings (either evangelical or liberal) is quite subversive in its very nature – you're transformed in the process.

> J: We'll see . . . In ritual studies, I remember when I was studying, reading that good ritual is ambiguous or multi-valent – that is, it functions in multiple ways. Perhaps that's another way of saying something similar? Is this also about trust as a curator – you create the space but then trust that people will do the work they need to do and trust that God will breathe in and through the gift that is offered by the team?

C: Probably the line I use most often in workshops is that the work of God is not only of human making. Coming from a liberal tradition, there's a temptation to assume that we need to do things on behalf of God; but while some things are of human making, there's a lot of stuff in faith that's not. I know what hasn't worked in my own life, and in the world I work and live in – people telling me I should have hope doesn't work, people telling me I should feel peace doesn't work. But the biblical stories about hope and peace don't begin with the end result; they talk about the acknowledgement of our humanity, of living with our fragility, of being honest about our weaknesses. So, with the spaces we try to honour our part in the process, and leave the rest to God.

I've been thinking recently about our temptation to try to become more like God – more holy, more sinless, more perfect. Perhaps the thing we should be working for is to become more human – more fragile, more vulnerable, more unfinished; to be better at being human. We try to give people a chance to be more human in a space; then it's up to God to do what God can do. It really feels risky and fragile and somewhat flimsy (I can't over-state that).

On a practical level, the spaces that work best seem to have layers that overlap but don't duplicate (music that doesn't say the same thing as the words; images that don't simply repeat the story being told). No layer is redundant. People have to work to make sense of it.

> **J:** One aspect of your approach that I am interested in is that you pull together a team for putting on art happenings four times a year or so. You are like an art collective. Lots of groups doing this sort of stuff are churches or communities and these happenings connect with their communal life and worship. I can see the strength in what you are doing – time and focus and creative energy. It appeals to me! Is that intentional or just the way it has happened? Do you think a community will grow out of it? Or is that a question you have not even entertained?

> **C:** Before Easter, one of the group members, Sam, suggested that we all have dinner together as a Holy Week moment, since we

weren't going to be doing an Easter space. I said, 'That sounds a lot like being a community,' and Sam replied, 'Maybe you just have to accept that we are one.'

There's a great freedom in not feeling the need to be a community, or not defining ourselves primarily as that. I think all of us are fairly connected to other primary communities that we love (although most of us aren't connected to other faith communities). It didn't feel like that was a big gap. And I think that if we'd focused on building community in the traditional ways, most of the group would have left the table under the guise of buying another drink and never returned from the front bar.

For the first year or two of basement spaces, the teams that curated the spaces were different each time, which was fun but hard work; it meant that we had to start with the basics each time. It was probably this time last year that we decided to get a little more intentional about meeting regularly, and to take group ownership of the spaces – and the core group self-selected into that (though the invitation is always open, and people do hang around the edges, which is great). I was very explicit at the time about this not being a community – I think that Christian community implies a lot of things (responsibilities) that we deliberately weren't going to do, and it implies a commitment that I knew a lot of the group weren't willing or able to make. But sometimes life takes over. There have been a few precipitative events this year that have made us responsive to each other in quite unexpected ways. We're being more human together, I guess – what we're doing in the spaces has become much more personal: less hypothetical (what they might need out there) and more immediate. Which is a bit scary on some levels . . .

So I think we're doing some of the things that community does. I don't know if that makes us community, and that's certainly not our primary definition. It wasn't our intention, and I don't think it ever will be (though I really can't speak for the others), but it would be lovely to think that in some unexpected way we're finding something about ourselves in doing this that we don't find elsewhere. What I can say is that it feels like we're stumbling into something lovely and remarkable together. It's really quite a gift to be part of it.

> J: I think there is such wisdom in letting some things just be natural – stumbling into something lovely – and if they don't work, no problem! It's made me think that often we (and I mean me as much as anyone else) in our enthusiasm are too hasty to shape or label or want to claim something for a group or see it as a new community or whatever, rather than let it be what it is. I really don't know what I can add to what you have said.

C: When we've had people from the public (those we haven't known) come into the spaces, they've avoided the parts of the space that are about community, or at least community as we've defined it. They seem drawn to the parts of a space that invite them to recognize their own story in the story that's being told around them . . . they don't need anyone to know their name, or where they've come from, or what they've done today. Maybe that's what community looks like for introverts, and that's who we're getting! That's not the same for everyone, of course, but we do often assume that people are lacking community. Perhaps what they're missing is resonance.

> J: I wonder if I can open up a new line of thought. I was amazed to read the word 'contextualization' in the book of interviews on curation by Hans Obrist.[3] It's such a missiology and theology word – I use it and love it (and have to come up with other accessible ways of talking about it). But it is so interesting to me that this is also an art question. I have been so inspired by you taking the worship curating you do into prisons. I know that you have done a mix of things there, but could you say something about how you even begin to think about curating in such a different context and community? I loved your use of Easter Saturday in the church

year as a moment of connection between the tradition and the context, for example.

C: I know now that when I start planning worship for prison, I have to go back inside to remember what it's like. The longer away from being inside that I am, the more abstract the reality becomes, and the more wrong I get it. When I go back in, and walk through the four security checkpoints, and the fingerprinting and iris checks, and begin to breathe the air, which is different in there, I start to think differently. I know immediately that the phrases or concepts or ideas that I've had floating around my head for worship won't work, and I wonder how I ever thought they would work. Life in there is so outside my reality that I can't hold its truth, as such, in my head.

I know that prison is a pretty extreme environment, but I think there's something true about that for everywhere. You have to breathe the air to know the space, before you can have any right to believe that you've got something relevant or transformative to offer, or to know what it is that needs to be transformed. The holy isn't something we transport into a place, it's something we uncover or point to.

So I know that the context changes the meaning of words and images. I think it also changes what we mean by worship, and certainly my theology. Stuff that's true outside isn't true inside, or it's true in a different way, so when I take a formed theology into prison, it's probably going to be wrong. When I take a process of theologizing inside – a faith that God has always spoken into and from within every culture and context, and will still do that, even in this one – then there's a chance that we might get something right. I use the traditions in which God has acted before, and the inherited wisdom about where to look for God, as hints, or as starting points (otherwise I'd have no idea, in prison, where to begin), and I tweak or rework them where they fall flat or are irrelevant. So, traditional prayers really don't work at all in prison, but the men writing psalms has been unexpectedly transformative.

When we use the processes within tradition and the Bible – the things that other people have done to encounter grace or healing – instead of the end results (the prayers or psalms or meaning they encountered), that seems to work.

One of the differences is that I've stopped thinking that in worship we should be spokespersons for God; instead I think we should be the spokespersons for the human experience. Which comes back to the idea that when we're at our most human we become most able to encounter God/the event of God.

Because I've realized how critical context is, I'm convinced now that I should only curate spaces for a group of people or a context that I know intimately. In fact, having to prepare worship for the general populace panics me a little now. The strange thing is that I've discovered that the more specifically contextual I am, the more accessible what we produce seems to be for people from a really wide range of contexts – but that's a lovely by-product, not an intention.

The other thing is that a lot of people in prison have nostalgic memories of church (even if they've never been!), and they don't like you playing with it. Religion is a comfort, a connection back to a time when things were OK. And I think we need to honour that, but also work with the tension that worship is somehow meant to be transformative as well, re-imagining the world as you described it before.

I think, as you've also said before, that at its heart alt worship invokes the trickster – and if anywhere needs the trickster it would be here – but perhaps the trickster is an inside joke to those who know and have power over the story. It simply doesn't work in prison.

At its purest, I guess the primary thing we are trying to offer is a moment of grace: a place to put our individual and unique human stories against a bigger story – finding the points of resonance, and the points of distinction, and saying that who we know ourselves as, in this place, is not all of who we are.

A couple of years ago, after a Christmas service, I realized that the most important part of worship or sacred space wasn't what happened in that time, but what that time made possible. While the liturgy was lovely, it wasn't in itself the transformative moment; that came in the ten minutes of unplanned silence after the service had finished. That silence probably wouldn't have been possible without the service, but it was the core bit of the service. So when I try to curate stuff now, I'm aware of it being a stepping stone to the main event, as such, which will be something that I can't manufacture.

In a practical sense, curating spaces for prison is like deciding to cook a soufflé without having any eggs. The prison population (these are big generalizations) thinks concretely not abstractly, has low levels of literacy and really short attention spans, has low capacity for metaphor and imagery. So the natural things to do would be tactile, and media-rich. But we can't take anything in to do that – no props (we can take in candles, but they have to be counted in and out, so not in large numbers), no media (apart from commercial CDs, and only then with the written authorization of the prison manager). We're limited pretty much to paper-based products (and even that can depend on the mood of whoever is on security) and ballpoint pens, which means that everything that traditional(!) alt worship relies on is impossible in prison.

All that is introduction to Easter this year. We did three days of worship/sacred space in the women's prison. Friday and Sunday were fairly traditional (although quite image- and music-based). On Holy Saturday, the Church traditionally doesn't worship – God is dead, there's nothing left to worship. In traditional versions of the Apostles' Creed, there's a line that says that Jesus descended to the dead, or to hell. If you talk to any prisoner, they'll talk about how prison is their hell, so it seemed the perfect day to do stuff in prison – the one day of the year that has the possibility of redeeming the experience of prison (and perhaps the one day of the year that redeems the Christian story, for those who are living in prison). Since printed images were the only visual media that seemed possible (at least that I've thought of yet), that's what we went with. We primarily used images that told the story, both of the human experience of hell (your lovely razorwire image, images from the bushfires), and of Jesus in hell (the Pietà, contemporary depictions). Alongside each of the images we had meditations that tried to connect the experience of being in prison with the story of Jesus going to hell.

We didn't do that lightly. I'm really aware that it's a risky thing, to invite people to 'enter into' their hell, as such, especially in such a context. But I think the only way for redemption or resurrection or restoration (or whatever other word we want to put to the transformation in faith) to happen is for us to go through that process that the biblical story talks about.

Some of the women loved it, some hated it. One funny thing that happened was that we had black sheets of card laid out on the floor with black pens, for the women to write responses or prayers onto, which no one else would be able to read. Outside prison we often use that kind of thing – it's a really nice way for people to be able to tell their story, and put it alongside someone else's, but to hold onto the stuff they can't make public. But as I moved around the room, I found women holding the cardboard up to the light and reading their prayers out to the other women next to them – we'd set up this group prayer thing that we could never have dreamed would happen (and if we'd tried to orchestrate it, I suspect that it would have been a disaster!).

I like it that the stakes are so high in prison – there are very few means of transformation in prison, and I like it that worship has the potential to be one of them. Bizarrely, because it seems almost impossible to do that, this gives a sense of liberation to what I try – we may as well give things a go. So I think I risk a lot more there. And the men and women are so incredibly gracious and generous and willing to risk things too . . . which makes a lovely change from working with groups that edge towards the cynical or hesitant.

Curating in public spaces

MARTIN POOLE

———◆———

Jonny: Martin, if there was an annual awards ceremony for alternative worship, your Advent Beach Huts would have got my vote for a Golden Globe or equivalent. It was such a great idea to turn beach huts into an Advent calendar – one hut with an installation or artistic piece inside being opened each day. It clearly caught the public imagination, the media loved it, and lots of people showed up on cold December evenings to take part. Whose idea was it, and how did the initial idea come about? Was it sparked by something else? Did it drop out of the sky? Did you fast and pray for 40 days?!

Martin: Thanks, but shouldn't it be the golden beach ball or Christmas bauble? As far as I remember the idea came up over dinner. We'd been beach-hut owners for seven or eight years and were having dinner with some friends who'd just bought one, and the idea just dropped into the conversation. In my experience it's pretty easy to have ideas, it's making them happen that is the hard part.

J: But it's such a good idea – I think those really good ideas aren't quite so common. When you say it just 'dropped' into conversation, surely it must have come from somewhere. Was there a conversation about doing worship/art in public space or is that an instinct you have developed to look for those sorts of things? I'm intrigued. Can you say something about how you proceeded from the idea to making it happen, which, as you say, is the hard part?

M: I think that good ideas start from little seeds of ideas that crop up all the time and you just have to know how to encourage them to grow. For me they're happening all the time – they can be a couple of words or a random comment; you just need to be able to recognize them. The Advent Beach Huts was part of a conversation about beach huts because our friends had just bought one, and someone said something about doors and advent calendars and my mind went racing from there. I wouldn't say I've developed an instinct for this but my spirituality leads me to try to recognize God everywhere and in everything I'm doing and provides the inspiration that not only fuels my faith but ends up being expressed in all these creative activities.

For me God is in everything, somehow, as the creative force behind it all, so any art events or show can be a source of inspiration. But I also find that ideas come from just walking down the street, because there's potential for something to pop into my head prompted by the buildings or the traffic or a poster or someone else walking along. The ideas rarely come from a conversation or discussion about worship, although we do brainstorm around topics for BEYOND events and come up with ideas for our programme as a group activity.

The test of a good idea is time; once the seed has germinated it needs time to develop and that's when you can find out whether it's a good idea or not. As you test it with others and start to work on it you soon get a sense of whether this is going to work. The response to the idea of the Beach Hut Advent Calendar was universally positive; once you said those four words to anybody their face would light up and they would smile and want to know more, so that was a positive sign. But there's still a lot of work that needs to go in to make something like this happen, and that's where an idea can either succeed or fail.

I think that you need to be very determined to make an idea happen and to really have the vision for it to succeed. Often we come up with an idea for BEYOND which on the face of it is impossible to achieve but with some application and perseverance it can eventually happen – possibly not in quite the way that you had envisaged, but the changes that occur during planning and production are part of what makes it fantastic. What keeps the idea moving forward is the vision for it in the first place – if that's strong enough you can achieve almost anything.

With the Beach Hut Calendar there was a lot of donkey work to do in getting it set up. This included leafleting all 450 beach huts along the Hove seafront to get owners to join in, arranging meetings to explain the idea to people, allocating dates to each hut, talking to each hut owner about its theme and what they'd like to do. In order for this to work practically I knew that we needed each hut to be responsible for its own creativity as there was no way our small team would be able to do 24 artworks, so the event became as much about encouraging ordinary people to be creative as it was about providing art for Brighton and Hove. In some cases the hut owners were happy for their hut to be used but wanted someone else to decorate it, while we had artists who wanted to create something but didn't have a hut, so we acted as liaison between these two groups to help this process along.

Then there's the design and printing of publicity and getting the message out about the event to TV and radio and local press, as well as distributing publicity so that people would come. Things can fall apart at any stage in the development of the idea and it's necessary to be really determined to make it succeed in order that the whole thing doesn't get derailed. Two days after launching the Easter Path in 2009, I discovered that one of the shops was unhappy with the art we'd put in their window and had removed it (despite lots of consultation beforehand). It would have been easy to just let that happen and for there to be a gap in the path at that point, but I was determined that we should find a solution, not just so that the path was complete but so that the shopkeeper felt good about what we were doing. So I spent a day working on new ideas and went back and presented some solutions to the shop, which they accepted. We carried on and they ended up being very happy with the event.

Thomas Edison said, 'Genius is 1 per cent inspiration and 99 per cent perspiration.' I think with God helping we can make the percentages a bit easier to cope with but there's definitely more work involved in making an idea happen than there is in having it in the first place.

J: You are in good company in doing lots of donkey work to make the events happen. Hans Obrist lists the tasks of administrator, amateur, author of introductions, librarian, manager, accountant, animator, conservator, financier, diplomat, guard, transporter, communicator and researcher as all roles the curator might take. It's not meant to be an exhaustive list – he's making the point that it is hard work and requires flexibility and a wide set of skills.[1] I found it reassuring that in the art world people are having to bust a gut to make things happen. It's not just in worship! Harold Szeeman, when asked by Obrist about the role of the curator, after pointing out the importance of flexibility, says, 'the most important thing about curating is to do with enthusiasm and love, with a little obsessiveness'.[2] I can see that enthusiasm and passion in what you are doing. I am thinking and talking with various people about curation in relation to worship. Is that a way you have thought about what you are doing? It seems to me that it is what you are doing, at least in relation to these public art events. Do you think that you will repeat the same events year on year and thus explore in different ways the same themes, which I am guessing might enable you to get some depth, or will you look to keep doing new events?

M: Subconsciously I have had curation in the back of my mind all the time but I didn't set out to make that my main objective. A few years ago I heard Mark Pierson at Greenbelt festival talking about curating worship and I was really taken with it. That was the first time I'd thought about that as a concept and it's been in the back of my mind ever since. Also, curation is the only practical way to do some things – there's no way we could produce 24 installations ourselves for the beach huts or even 12 for the Easter Path, and certainly one of BEYOND's aims has always been to encourage others' creativity. It seems to me that finding something spiritual through creativity doesn't just work as an observer and is more powerful if you can be involved in the creative act yourself – then we're reflecting something of the nature of God within us. That's why most BEYOND events have some interactive element to them so that people who attend have to do something themselves.

There's tension for me in the balance between curation and creation – I like to create as well and see the organization of these events as a creative act. I also can't stop myself from throwing my own ideas into the overall. I think the best exhibitions are the ones that come with a point of view or that have a spin put on them by the curator that makes you think differently about the work. I definitely agree that you have to have a passion and a certain amount of obsession to do this, otherwise you'd never have the energy to see them through – there are so many hurdles to jump on the way to completing something.

It's interesting to realize that even after only one year, BEYOND is beginning to develop a routine and we are starting to revisit some events. Our July event in 2008 was the Fingermaze meditation, which we then translated to Greenbelt, and this year we're going back to the original Fingermaze in Hove Park and will do something different, but based on last year. I think we'd be lynched if we didn't do the Beach Hut Advent Calendar again, it was so popular. And there are many things about it that we could do better this year. This also applies to the Easter Path. So we already have a shape to our year which we could continue on for ever – which goes against the ethos of BEYOND, which was always to be experimenting. Maybe we need to set up another organization to take over successful events and run them regularly while BEYOND carries on innovating? I know we could do each of these big events bigger, better and with more focus – the challenge is getting the resources to be able to do that and we're beginning to think about ways we might do that right now. But I don't want to lose the focus on new events as well and continuing to innovate and experiment.

> J: You mention curation and creation – Laura Drane describes the artist-curator, which I suspect is what you are. I'm glad to hear that you are repeating things like the beach huts – I think you will find new depth by lingering with some things. How you balance and do everything and stay fresh, I don't know! How did you get into this? Were your reference points through other worship communities or through contemporary art or both?

M: My background is fairly creative, since I've been an actor and then a TV producer for graphics and design for most of my working life, and I've always tried to bring that into my worship life. It seems to me that we worship a wonderful creative God and I'm sure he wants us to be creative in the way we respond to him. It's slightly mystifying to me that more often than not our worship is formulaic and ritualized and uses forms of words and actions that are alien to most people who have never had any contact with church. I also believe that God speaks through creativity anywhere and I'm just as likely to find him in the latest exhibition at the Tate Modern (and sometimes more likely) than I am at my parish church or in a cathedral somewhere.

To go back to your original question, I guess I don't have any reference points for this except a desire to communicate God's love in new, meaningful, symbolic ways that make people sit up and take notice. As far as I'm concerned, anything goes in terms of how we do that.

> J: If you lead worship as a traditional priest you get some training in liturgy and leading services. If you lead worship as a band there are conferences and courses and books. But if you curate there's very little out there, and it's potentially a much more complex set of things to negotiate and manage. One discussion I had recently with someone was about how

you nurture good practice of curation in others, how you pass on the skills. In the community this person is part of they have quite a few new people who are taking on the role. But they seem to have services or experiences that are full of content by way of ideas and theory and the services often end up being more like workshops than worship, with too much presentation of the ideas. It reminds me a little bit of an earlier phase in Grace where there were often too many words and not enough space for encounter. It's still a danger sometimes. Less is often more. In art and worship people want moments of epiphany where a connection is made, where the soul is moved, the presence of God is sensed, as opposed to just thinking that that was a nice set of ideas we explored at some rational level.

What sort of process do you have in BEYOND as you put together worship or installations? How have you helped develop that skill in and with others in the team? And how do you then manage the mix of exploring ideas with opening up the possibility of encounter, of leading people to worship, of enabling those epiphanies to take place?

M: We try to keep in mind all the time that the encounter comes from God, not us – we're just there to create an environment where that can happen. I'm quite against the idea that we try to dictate to people what they should think about a particular theme or activity, and try always to keep in mind the fact that Jesus often didn't explain his parables but just put them out there and let people draw their own conclusions.

We do have a process for developing our ideas, which starts with us meeting at the beginning of the month to kick around ideas. This is a very blue-sky thinking session with no boundaries and no aim at an outcome. We range from talking about the theology behind our chosen theme through to stupid games that we think might be useful. I tend to go straight for the practical ideas, whereas others are much better at focusing on the spiritual side. It's very stimulating, quite like a very intellectual Bible study discussion, and we all get quite a lot out of this. After that I write up some notes and circulate them to everyone. Sometimes people then contribute more ideas by email. We then meet two weeks later, once the ideas have had a chance to settle down in our minds and mature. We try to shape the programme for the event from that, so that by the end of this meeting we have a rough idea of what is going to happen and can allocate some tasks associated with it. That usually gives us a week to prepare stuff, which is sometimes a bit tight.

For the larger events such as the Beach Hut Calendar and Easter Path there has to be a longer lead time and the idea tends to be pretty well formed as soon as we've had it, so it's a more administrative process that mostly falls onto me – which is why we're looking for a volunteer worker to help with the next one.

In terms of managing encounter – I'm not sure we do that particularly. In the spirit of experimentation that we've always had, we're experimenting all the time with how that happens. The latest Fingermaze turned out to be a great opportunity for people to encounter things that were quite unexpected from our point of view. Our only rule, if you like, is to make sure that people 'do' something at some point and we often try to give time for discussion as well, although this should never replace the doing. So I guess our belief is that encounter comes through active doing. It seems odd to me when you look at the average church service and realize how passive people are, even when it's a Eucharist, which should be the ultimate act of 'doing'. There isn't any other activity in life where we're expected to sit and listen for an hour or more – even school lessons are not like that these days. I suppose that's why church is so keen on singing because it is at least a participatory activity, although I find more and more that it's difficult to participate because the songs are not known to me and I dread to think what it feels like to those who've never been to church or sung any kind of hymn!

I think the key to it for me is not to try to manipulate the encounter to get a particular outcome. Just because I understand that a cross shape made out of dirty tissues says something about sin and atonement doesn't mean that I can expect everyone to realize that. I just need to trust that through the image God will teach each person something about him- or herself that will be appropriate for them. It's a true form of parable, where we just 'tell the story' and let the participants draw their conclusions themselves. I guess I'm saying the epiphany needs to come from God, not us.

> J: The most recent piece of public art/worship of yours that I encountered was a huge ice sculpture with things buried in it at Greenbelt festival, which created a lot of interest and responses. What was the idea behind this and how did you reflect on people's sometimes violent interactions with the sculpture?

M: This came from thinking about the Greenbelt theme – 'Standing in the Long Now'. I came to a worship-group brainstorm with a whole bunch of very rough ideas for things that we could do around the site, as Ben Edson had asked me to think about that following our Fingermaze labyrinth the previous year. I had loads of ideas, from little peephole worship boxes placed around the site to laser displays on the hill above the campsite, and right at the end a vague idea about a block of ice with things frozen in it, which would melt over the weekend, which I threw in as an afterthought. As we talked around the ideas all the other suggestions got thrown out or dismissed as being too difficult, until to my surprise we were left with the ice sculpture which somehow seemed to be the most feasible of them all!

I went away to try to work out how feasible it really was. I started by buying a chest freezer on eBay and experimented with various size blocks of ice in crates or plastic bags with a motley collection of things in them. My wife went spare when I rolled up with this freezer, which I proposed to keep in the garden until

I managed to find a way to hide it in our shed. The results were less than impressive – misshapen, grey blocks of ice that you couldn't see through and melted in about half a day – so I started looking for companies that could do this for me.

The first quote I got was for a bigger block of ice than we eventually ended up with, but cost £25,000! At that point I really began to wonder about the feasibility of this, but I persevered. Eventually one of the ice companies I kept calling up asking for different quotes got fed up and gave me the contact details of their supplier in Kent. He turned out to be a great guy, who had also started his business by buying old freezers and experimenting, so he knew where I was coming from. His standard block of ice was only £30 and by constructing our sculpture mostly out of standard blocks we were able to keep the whole cost, including delivery to Greenbelt, down to £500.

The day it arrived was so exciting – we offloaded the ton-and-a-half block with a forklift and started to unwrap it. At first it was a bit disappointing as the ice was very cloudy, but we realized that this was just condensation. As we poured water over it the surface cleared and we were left with this beautiful, clear, one-metre cube of ice, with a one-and-a-half metre spire containing a statue of Jesus that appeared to be floating in mid-air – it was more beautiful than I could ever have imagined. As the ice began to melt the whole thing became covered with a stream of flowing water running down the structure.

We had suspended a number of items inside the block, including 25 perspex crosses, a number of rosaries and some sunflowers, with the idea that these should be gradually revealed to the open air as the ice melted. What we hadn't accounted for was the impatience of youth! After a few hours groups of teenagers began to chip away at the ice to try to get the things inside. Over the next day or so this escalated, until kids were bringing toffee hammers and stones, and eventually concrete blocks, to chip away the ice. Periodically people would clear them off but they would always come back and by Sunday the beautiful ice sculpture had turned into a misshapen block of grey ice that had been rolled off its plinth and lay in a big patch of mud.

A lot of people got quite upset about this, especially in our team who had seen all the work that went into creating it, but I felt quite differently. Our aim with this kind of art is to provoke a response and we certainly got that. It's not our job to try to control or predict that response, because hacking it to pieces with a hammer is just as valid as sitting quietly and watching it melt. Also, this was an ice sculpture – it was always meant to disappear, it was a transient artwork. The kids just helped that process along a little quicker. There was also a deep spiritual lesson to be learned: to some people this spoke of Jesus suffering on the way to the cross, the way he was beaten and abused and damaged. That's an interpretation we could never have predicted and has a much more powerful spiritual dimension to it than I could ever have imagined.

Ben Edson, who co-ordinated the worship at Greenbelt that this was part of, went on to write a really interesting story on his blog about this, putting himself in the position of the curator wanting to protect the artwork and have people understand what we had meant by it originally, and myself as the artist who was happy that people were responding somehow, even if it wasn't what we predicted. I feel uncomfortable describing myself as an artist and prefer the curator title and role, but it's clear that there is a fine line between these two and that both are important.

Depth a close friend but not a lover

DAVE WHITE

———•◆•———

Jonny: Dave, as I understand it you have curated a Stations of the Cross exhibition in Hamilton public gardens, New Zealand, and before that in other venues, for several years now. I really hope I get to come one year but the stories and photos look amazing. How did you get into this?

Dave: As a young kid I used to make obstacle courses for the kids on my street on a Saturday morning. We had a quarter-acre backyard, and anything I found I would make into some challenge for the local boys. So, they would have to use hockey sticks to get balls up compost piles into garden tunnels. I'd make kids go under stuff, and over anything, and through and up and around whatever I could find in the garage. And then I'd turn the hose sprinkler on and finish with a water slide. That was followed by sessions of insane 'jackass' style cross-country croquet. Hoops in unsuspecting places. That was the beginning of my creative urge and the sense of fulfilment of providing experiences for others.

Later I learned guitar and played in bands and rocked traditional Youth for Christ rallies in Hamilton and around the country. Then I got to produce monthly evangelistic productions in Hamilton – a standard concoction of drama, song and dance with altar call and response.

Then I went teaching. Then I left teaching.

And then I had an epiphany at a Stations of the Cross exhibition in Auckland curated by Mark Pierson. I thought it magical, sublime, and have invested much energy into curating similar experiences for others. It's still just really obstacle courses for my neighbours – just with a kingdom of God twist.

J: Do you think that by sticking with the same narrative/event over a long period, that has enabled you to go deeper with it than if you'd done it once and then done something else?

D: 'Deeper with it' isn't a bad phrase. Deeper in the sense that shallowness around something like Stations of the Cross is only avoided over time, and multiple excursions. The viewers, some who have made it a traditional yearly venture, need awareness to slow down, to journey with the narrative and installation. To allow the mystery to sink a little. Punters outside the faith (or catholic faith especially) need multiple excursions to get it if they come. Every year too it gains credibility in the art community and the public – for just being a significant art event on the calendar. For the artists, yes, indeed. Each year we as a Stations collective of artists have to revisit the Scripture and seek a fresh angle for which to communicate the cross. We have had growth over five years from 300 to 3,000. That means 'deeper' pockets have to fund it too. If we had done something else, than we would have lost the momentum in untold ways that each year brings. Being of stubborn mind is important to sustain this mission – to further the goal of engaging the Passion of Christ with the numbness of our local community.

J: In relation to the future of curation, one of the themes that I touch on in Part One is continuity. Here's a quote from Simon Sheikh:

Repetition could be transformed into continuity literally doing the same in order to produce something different not in the products but in the imagination. I propose working on a ten-year plan constantly doing the same exhibition with the same artists. Imagine this: constantly asking the same artists to contribute to the same thematic exhibition thus going into the depths of the matter rather than surfing the surface. Indeed going off the deep end as it were by refusing the demands for newness.[1]

It was reading that essay that got me thinking about depth in relation to what you do. I had been thinking about it from the artist's point of view but I like what you are saying about the returning public. Do you work with the same artists each year or is there a regular core with some change?

D: I have been thinking a bit more about depth. Deeper, I think, has some tension in respect to the tension of being honest to the narrative. Deeper can imply abstract. It can imply richness, but also depth that can drown. Deep is OK if you can swim. Yes – over the years we have attained some depth but it is also with some commitment to the narrative of the Easter story. In the early years of Stations of the Cross, as a missional experience – in a public space with an invitation to the public – 'depth' had to be curated with much care and wisdom. The heart of the Stations is telling a story that is profound. And by telling we mean experiencing.

The Easter story must be left in lots of way to fend/welcome/stir for itself, as it has done for centuries. I caution artists as they meditate on the Scripture to expose both their artistic imagination and spirit leanings with reverence to the narrative. A viewer must be stirred by the big picture – a story of confounded, inexplicable salvation that somehow makes kingdom sense.

This is not to say that I'm anti 'depth'. Artistic integrity and the avoidance of shallow art propaganda are also well-travelled dictates of the Stations collective. Artistic imagination can't overshadow the beauty of the Passion. It would be very interesting to allow artists absolute free reign but I'm not sure that a non-Jesus follower will be any the wiser or closer to the river of life. For us, 'depth' is a close friend but not a lover. 'Story' should be the lover. Depth is just a natural result of being repetitive. Any collection of people revisiting Scripture cannot possibly read it, imagine it and be mundane, boring, shallow. We work with the same core of five or six artists – with revolving artists (they do one every two or three years) and one-off freshies.

J: I was interested to read that you revisit the narrative, the story, together through Scripture and looking to uncover fresh things – can you say a bit more about how that has happened? Are there particular things that have cracked open the story again for you?

D: Our process is one of dialogue in a collective environment. We intentionally try to break down the individual artist concept – from inspiration, design, creation and exhibition. Our collective asks each artist interested in Stations to dream of installations for all 15 stations. They have one sheet of paper to scribe their thoughts for each station. At any meeting of the collective we throw around three stations only.

These individual pieces are brought to the table and negotiated, mocked, discussed and prayed. Sometimes an idea mutates with the collective involvement into something worthy. Sometimes an artist's original idea is farmed out to another artist. Artists sometimes work collaboratively.

The collective inefficient toil is valuable for its depth of discussion and theological insights as well as the usual chaos that happens when you get a group of artists in a room. Depth occurs when people meditate on the Scripture . . . and so-called winning ideas by an individual are critiqued by others for their shallow representation. Depth occurs when people bring their own Christological views to the Passion stations. The depth gets shared among us – as people start dishing it out (for and against)!

J: I love the phrase, 'Depth is a close friend but not a lover. Story should be the lover.' I think that would probably be a challenge to the way some people plan who love the artistic, creative side of things, love what they sense is going on in culture and get it to fit with the story; you are suggesting a much more humble posture towards the narrative even if you are questioning or reading the text from another angle. I have always liked that when I have sensed it in the air in communities. I get asked quite often about how the Bible is used or functions in alternative worship, because there isn't the usual didactic teaching. And at its best I think it is when there is this communal engagement and wrestling with the Scriptures but in a way that wants to do so with reverence. In Grace, the community I am part of, I think that we have found some sort of depth when we have lingered with a theme such as hospitality for a season and let the Scriptures challenge us. I have found your comments very helpful personally. I will work on my own posture a bit and try to let the story be the lover.

I also love the notion of collective inefficient toil. Our culture is maxed out. Everyone is too busy, working too hard and there's this pressure on time always (maybe it's worse in London?). So worship and art stuff often ends up needing some kind of efficiency – it's horrible! I'm sure that you get efficient when it comes near the time of delivering the Stations, but that stage of time-wasting together and knocking ideas around isn't done enough in my experience, though I know it's always fruitful. I'm talking to myself here!

I have never visited the Stations in Hamilton and I expect lots of people who read this interview won't have either. Could you perhaps lift the lid on a couple of moments or stations that have stood out for you?

D: One of the finer stations when it was curated in a gallery space was the crucifixion. We set the room up very beautifully, very luxurious. It was a large space. The back walls had this luminescent material lit with very fine lights and pure, soothing and magical kind of curtaining around the walls. In the centre of the space was a white bath on a large raised platform. There was a red carpet leading to the bath and a red velvet stool placed to one side of the bath. The bath had a shower overhead. In the bath, unseen, was a red fluid that recycled through the shower head back into the bath. The pump was connected to a sensor – so the pumping 'blood bath' only turned on for any individual or group as they came closer to the bath. The audio track used was the theme from *Schindler's List*, which has a haunting violin melody combined with a very spare rhythmic soldier-ish drum beat. It was a stunning piece. Rich theologically from many perspectives, quite barbaric, but also with this very magical wondrous beauty. It was a very strong image.

Another one that sticks in the mind was the station where Jesus carries the cross. From a street-type ice cream cart, a woman in a white coat offers an ice cube with a curious greenish centre. You take it. You hold the ice cube in the palm of your hand, your fingers curled around it on a cold autumn evening; it melts painfully in your palm, leaving a moist leaf cut in the shape of the cross, as you journey the path. That is an engaging experience of Jesus carrying the cross. It's personal, experiential, creative. And the leaf is from our back yards. Our back yards. Christ's bearing of the cross is for Kiwis in the South Pacific too. But this station, in 2008, was all the above but true to the narrative.

And then a cherry-picker, the biggest in town, was used to create a 'halo' of angels suspended in the night sky in circular 'umbrella' style. It was large-scale, impressive, angel after angel cut in white vinyl, some performing the Maori haka, a war dance. In a rectangular garden, below the halo, was a single cut-out figure, floating head down, a knife in his back. The Scripture this installation amplified was where Christ says to the Roman guards that at any time he could call an army of angels to his defence. The sheer scale, this maze of angels overhead, the sense of Christ's humility, his loneliness, his commitment to smallness and non-violence, was overwhelming.

J: Thanks for these three 'moments'. They are gorgeous and poignant. I am interested in the sometimes small but powerful connections you make with your context, like the New Zealand leaf. I remember seeing a slide you showed of the crucifixion station represented as a washing line with bloodied children's clothes on it – a highly controversial representation that related to a horrendous story of a murder in New Zealand that year.

How did you manage to negotiate being in such a public space?

D: I took the proposal to the public-garden manager with a prayer and a 'you having a laugh?' kind of self-doubt. I was surprised myself to be allowed to use the gardens. Praise Jesus. The gardens are not open after hours to the public, so technically it's a private hire of the gardens. They were hesitant in the first year, with a large bond paid up front. The management is very supportive now, after three years of exhibitions, though the gardeners themselves dislike us very much. The odd leaf does get disturbed. What may not be clear is that each night we set out and pack up 15 installations, and all the lighting that goes with it! The whole shebang. It is quite insane, yet achievable. We have two hours, from 6 p.m. to 8 p.m., to haul lighting and art pieces from the HQ tents and container into the 15 spaces. From 8 p.m. to 10 p.m. the public can experience Stations of the Cross. At 10 p.m. it all goes back to HQ. This sounds disturbingly intense. And it is. But it's also a good communal experience – beating the clock, working together. Night after night for seven nights. One punter came back to the gardens in daylight – just to check, because he would not believe that this is what we did!

Gifts from the edge of chaos

NIC HUGHES AND KESTER BREWIN

Jonny: It made me smile when you told me that you had someone come in to do the Belbin management test at a Vaux weekend on the various characters in a team, and you found that you were nearly all 'plants' – people who throw monkey wrenches into the system, make mischief, love creative ideas. You were an unusual group in that respect, brimming with talent and ideas, but what on earth was it like trying to get such a group of artists to produce anything? Was curation a model and was that done by one person or a group?

Nic: That's true, the majority of us had cancerous potential – we'd eat ourselves given half a chance. It worked well when these energies operated against aspects of church orthodoxy; it was more painful when we turned the same critiques back on our own entrenchments. We were a broad church, coming from very different denominations of practice. We experimented with various organizational models, the main ones being producers or art directors (both curatorial, as it happens). I've just got to mention Open Space Technology, I've been thinking about it a lot. Open space is a great way of leading to ideas generation. One of the four principles is, 'Whoever comes is the right people'; it's an act of collaborative 'make do' – you make do with the given resources, respect the ecosystem. I might add, we never did this at Vaux – if we had, there might have been a greater number of happier people.

J: Most groups planning worship are probably more open space than groups of artists creating exhibitions, perhaps?

That is, anyone can join the community and there can be people in a creative team who you might not have chosen. Managing that blend is a skill or challenge, I think, to help those who are newer to the process learn and contribute while drawing on the more experienced members of the group. It probably ends up being some kind of balance. I think 'whoever comes is the right people' is quite a radical statement in terms of art production. Do you really believe that, Nic? I wonder if it might be good to think about different kinds of event – some truly open space in this way, but some where you do select a particular team to work with.

N: Yes, I'm committed to those four principles of open space. 'Whoever comes is the right people' is so appropriate for diverse, creative organisms. The thing is, I *did not* believe this when Vaux was operating. A U-turn! I wish I had! ☺

Kester: What was it like trying to get such a group of artists to produce anything? Everything from very easy to impossible. I think in some ways what we did was good because there actually was quite a lot of slack. Nic, you may disagree with this, but my feeling is that things went best when the curative element was quite light touch: we met at the beginning of the process, threw ideas around, and then went our separate ways and created stuff that we then put together towards the end. In terms of curating the space, we did our best to set things up . . . but then Jon (another key Vaux member, and working artist) would inevitably turn up with half an hour to go and rearrange the whole space. Frustrating, but it was invariably right.

I also think that there's an element of myth about how much required curation. Very often it was only three or four elements that really needed fitting together. There were occasions when it was like herding cats, but those were the exception rather than the rule, and we were generally just pretty pleased to have whatever people offered.

As to the nature of the curation that was done – despite our pretences at flat structure, there was a very clear hierarchy of influence. Basically Nic and I, and later Jon, were there to try to do some kind of quality control. Perhaps that was the hardest element. Curating good stuff is easier than having to find ways of not allowing amateurish contributions to take over too much. The really good ideas don't come along quite as often as the sloppy ones. So the easier moments were when the ideas were flowing well among those who knew their art. Much harder coming up with a service when the muse has gone, and people start coming up with basically terrible ideas. Or is that too harsh?

N: I agree, a light touch is vital for any 'redirective practice'. I like to see it in terms of reducing the 'design footprint', or as in Sun Tzu's *The Art of War*: deploying minimum interventions for big results (détourner, swerve or divert a system), having the ability to 'elegantly' redirect large bodies or systems. Structure and transparency was a real problem. Some of us wanted flat, others (me at the time) wanted more hierarchy. This was compounded by the fact that we never fully resolved as a group how Vaux should be. Looking back, things would have been a lot easier if we'd worked out a command structure – one way or the other.

This notion of 'terrible' and 'good' is interesting. Again, at the time it was a preoccupation of mine. There was a clash of values. Did the group hold inclusion and participation as the highest value, or did we value quality and high standards of production? Are they mutually exclusive? It all depends what the desires and intentions of the collective are. Open Space Technology can help resolve some of these tensions. As a group, Vaux never really fully resolved this or communicated exactly how it wanted to operate.

J: 'Things went best when the curative element was quite light touch' – I like that. I think that's my sense too. Though I have noticed in Grace that there are what you might call a number of curator styles or approaches. The light touch seems

Nic Hughes and Kester Brewin

to me to be the ability to hold the space open for ideas and not resolving things too quickly in a planning process. How did the process of creating ideas work in Vaux? I'm interested in the germ of an idea – for example, Concrete Liturgies, the process of creating ideas around it, how those are then sifted or shaped and moulded to create an articulation, and then the set-up, which you have touched on already?

K: I think the ideas creation process was organic and 'emergent' in the sense that it depended on people reading/discovering interesting stuff, and other people bouncing connections off that. The whole dirt theme that we explored at Vaux came from Nic passing a battered photocopy of a text (it turned out to be Lewis Hyde's *Trickster Makes This World*) saying that he thought I'd probably get something out of it. That intuitive sense of what is going to feed someone else doesn't happen without a lot of prior interaction. I took the text, then went on to his other books, while Nic and others then responded in turn to ideas I brought back to them.

So the germ could literally be anything. The Concrete Liturgies idea came out of Timmy Bayes getting into concrete as part of his artistic exploration, and then us looking at stuff Tadao Ando had done with concrete churches and tying that up with our urban bent. At least, that's my memory of it.

N: Though Vaux hinted at the possibility of a curatorial model of worship, it didn't really implement it. I don't think we perceived ourselves this way. I wish we had – we'd look well clever now! The thing is, retrospectively you can apply a curatorial gloss to our practices and it begins to make a lot of sense. A transparent, fully theorized model of curation may have made the experience of Vaux radically different. There again, maybe we needed the disequilibrium and turbulence to retrieve gifts from the 'edge of chaos'? Invariably what we did was more the result of accident than design. Maybe that was part of the frustration? It was a space that accidentally produced design, rather than a space designed to produce accidents. The latter is far more preferable. That would be a place designed to curate error. Put another way, a space design to foster synergy and emergent behaviour.

It might be worth talking about a few actual examples – perform an autopsy on the corpse. My three favourite Vaux moments: curation and collaboration.

1 *The 'inverted lift' from the Beautiful Imperfection service at Greenbelt.* As a way of introducing the sacraments we used two dancers. It proved to be a piece of spine-chilling non-verbal liturgy. One dancer carried the other upside-down towards the altar. The inverted dancer's arms were outstretched, cruciform. There had been conversation as to the function and position of the dance within the wider service, what it was meant to achieve and how it might relate to the controlling meta-idea. However, the details and mechanics of the piece were left up to the dancers – we let them do what they do best. The result was this unexpected, out-of-the-blue inverted lift. It still chokes me when I think about it today – talk about short-circuiting language!

In this example I think authorship lies with the group (kind of). The group had determined the umbrella idea and the dance formed an assemblage alongside various other pieces of creative liturgy. This particularly intense moment would not have existed if a network of now long-forgotten 'actors' had not surrounded it. One cannot separate the dance from the collaborative work of the group, the backdrop of the festival and a thousand other complex threads and narratives. In other words, one cannot identify a specific curator, apart from a fuzzy, nebular mass of influences.

There is some sort of curation apparent, a standing back and withdrawing, letting the dancers create. However, there is also the all-important context, the network that holds it in place. This is less to do with curation and more to do with

relational and interactive productions of space – maybe curation, collaboration and flux?

2 *The spectacle of a ripped curtain.* Again, a wonderful example
of non-verbal liturgy, positioned within an Easter service at
St Peter's. This time I think the event was post-communion
and a huge floor-to-ceiling curtain (that had hung throughout
the service) suddenly split and collapsed. The symbolism is
quite blatant, a re-enactment of the ripping temple curtain after
the death of Christ.

As with the previous example, I suspect the splitting curtain
is held within its own liturgical web or assemblage. There would
have been various mixed-media inputs and contribution, including communion, leading up to the event. As usual, Vauxites
(or Vauxiles) would have been 'invited' to forage for their
own meanings: discover shards and fragments for themselves,
make connection and edit their own service. Everyone would
leave with different traces and threads, their own meanings –
a kind of wiki-worship or chaotic-fiction. If there is curation,
it might be understood by the 'lightness of touch' and enough
space to make connection.

3 *The act of desecration in D1 (the Dirt Service).* I love this service!
The incident in mind was the smashing of the elements towards
the end of the Dirt Service. Again, I think there had been
several contributions, all reflecting on the meta-idea of 'dirt'.
We moved towards communion, where at some point the elements were treated quite violently. I can't remember who did
it or how it was exactly done. What I do remember is Vanessa
restoring them back on the table. It was amazing, profound and
deeply moving. We never planned this, predicted this or spoke
about this beforehand. We knew we would trash the sacraments,
but we hadn't really worked on any exit strategy. A classic case
of Vaux black-boxism! The services were a series of disconnected points, of key moments surrounded by huge voids. We
closed the voids together, with whoever was there at the time.
Vanessa just reacted to the moment: pure synergy. Maybe that's

how we worked: set up situations, didn't think too much about them, worked with the elements at hand, busked it – a form of improvised worship.

The black-box and the unknown mechanisms within the box were where the act of curation occurred. Maybe I was initially wrong, and we could only make 'accidentally produced design'; if we got good at it and formalized it, all the beauty would have been destroyed. Like all good design, we were always 'out of control'.

K: 'Vaux hinted at the possibility of a curatorial model of worship, it didn't really implement it.' Yes, I'd totally agree with this. We actually talked a lot about it, and did occasionally appoint 'curators' for services, but I don't think we were emotionally ready for that as artists. It is possible, as Nic says, to apply a retrospective gloss of curation, but it wasn't quite there fully.

But I agree again – it was the chaos that actually gave us something important. I have been thinking quite a bit about ruptures recently. Paul's conversion, Peter's vision . . . there are lots of examples of transformations that occurred that were experienced as chaotic and heretical. It's easy to underestimate just how violently against their orthodoxy – and all the cultural baggage and belonging that went with that – these ruptures were. And while in retrospect, or from the divine perspective, we might perceive them as curated, to those involved they must have appeared chaotic . . . where were they going to hit solid ground? So I now wonder if in a way Vaux's part of the puzzle was to be one such rupture – for us, and for the Church in general. I've certainly never recovered – but would I want to go back? Sometimes, yes – but not necessarily to the chaos. It's very tiring living in that chaotic space, artistically and theologically.

To explain a little about those pieces Nic highlighted.

The inverted lift: this was part of a service/series of developing services around the idea of the 'walking wounded' – the church as a field hospital, almost. I wouldn't take that view so much now, but it was right for us then. Over a building piece of music, with a video-projected background, Merve Broughton and Esther Baker performed a dance. They had had very little time to choreograph something to go exactly with the video, but there was real serendipity in how it turned out. This is why curation is often best light touch – it allows for these serendipitous moments to break through. It's also why it can be a real blessing if people don't know all that is going to go on. I had had no involvement in the video or the dance, but it just *worked*.

The ripped curtain was a similar moment. Various people were involved in setting it up – a huge piece of red fabric, very lightly sewn down the middle, was hung across the whole chancel. Again, dance was involved. We had done a liturgy all about Easter, but then this dance happened and no one could have predicted that the ripping from top to bottom of this 'curtain' would happen the way it did: the tension of being hung up there meant that with the slightest pull . . . it near exploded as it tore itself apart and the dancers came through it.

For the D1 dirt service: basically, having explored some pretty iconoclastic ideas, we then had the elements set up on a pure white cubic altar. As the communion liturgy was read out, at the bit where it talked about 'this is my body, broken for you', Jon just dropped the loaf, carefully cut, which smashed on the altar. He then lifted a wine glass full of red wine and dropped that too. It was violent, and profoundly shocking. A rupture that was curated, to get people to experience something of the original shock of the crucifixion, and to explode the way that we have sanitized it in our communion liturgies. Again, very few people in the group knew it was going to happen, and those who did had not thought it entirely through – which was a good thing. So, as we all sit there with these bits of bread everywhere and broken glass and pools of wine, there's just this silence while everyone thinks, 'What the hell do we do now?' But Vanessa gently got up and restored the elements to the table, which was extremely moving, a sort of Mary Magdalene moment.

So there was an element of planning and curation, I guess, in each of these, but not too much to squeeze the life out of it. 'If we got good at it and formalized it, all the beauty would be destroyed.' Spot on.

N: Nic Bourriaud's got this lovely quote in *Postproduction*: 'Notions of originality (being at the origin of) and even creation (making something from nothing) are slowly blurred in this new cultural landscape marked by the twin figures of the DJ and the programmer.'[1]

Remixing (or editing or sampling) material that already has been made is an act of production. It's now part of how we understand ourselves. For me, the patron saint of curatorial activity is Marcel Duchamp: his recontextualization of a men's urinal into an art gallery was landmark. From there on, one can trace various eruptions of essentially the same activity throughout the twentieth century; for instance, Gysin/Burrough's 'Cut-ups', the situationist's 'détournement', punk's 'bricolage', hip-hop's sampling, and today the presence of 'mash-up'.

I wanted to offer the notion of curation as 'steering' or 'swerving'. As cultural practitioners we only ever rearrange other people's ideas and work: we curate or corral the pieces into different patterns. Powerful effects like 'context' and 'use' will tend to kick in and generate new meaning.

I think you're bang-on in terms of the relationship of curation to imagination and world-building. Maturana and Varela say, 'Every reflection brings forth a world,'[2] and it's a fantastic statement. The idea of worship as 'terra-forming' (birthing planets) is fascinating. I use this statement a lot when I'm teaching typography or identity-building. Designers essentially construct worlds and cosmologies.

J: Rewinding a little, I wanted to come back to your 'conversion', Nic, from hierarchy/control to collaboration/ participation. I think this move is good, and movements in art that do that always inspire me. But are there limits to this – it is a nice theory to teach, but frustrating in practice. The 'font fascism' approach (as you described yourself in a question time at Greenbelt one year!) meant a particular aesthetic that you just don't get in the same way with total open planning. Put bluntly, would you now have let anyone have an equal contribution? Isn't there something about gift that needs to be recognized – that there were some very strong gifts in Vaux and it was good that they were used? Sure, the balance would change drastically if you rewound. But doesn't curation, albeit light touch, need to take place precisely to help exclude and include minimally, to nudge and shape and swerve, as you put it, to create a particular vision of the world?

I was talking with Laura Drane, who works commissioning exhibitions and the like, and she was saying that there are a whole number of styles and approaches to curation and some are frankly a nightmare to work with – just as controlling as any other kind of leading. So there is, no doubt, a dark side, as you say. It all depends what you mean. But I think that's why it's important to have these conversations, and questions. What do we mean? What is a good set of instincts? How do you keep light touch but maintain a vision? How do you allow room for chaos, as you suggest?

I wanted to ask you guys about the limits or the edge. There's a piece in *Curating Subjects* that is about 'curating beyond the canon'. This really interests me. In the art world there is a trade-off or set of negotiations between the institutions, the curator, the artists, the public, and the world of art and its own traditions. Curators need to be able to be true and hold their integrity. Some end up in a museum, say. Others decide to be freelance – you can see the parallel with being in a church denomination (or cathedral even, as some are) or out on the edges. My view is that it's good news when you have good people in both these spaces simultaneously – that's how newness comes. Vaux chose to be outside of the institution, although you met in its space – perhaps in and out at the same time? Was this important to you or just the way it happened? And you messed with things – words, dirt, language, the bread and wine – in the spirit of the trickster, offending some and inspiring others. Some art seems to be about reconfiguring the historical canon and some curators love that play – I think that there is a side to Vaux that might be about reconfiguring the canon? And perhaps about raising questions in terms of where the canon is read from or who has the right to read it, even? It's to do with a prophetic imagination, and art and prophecy are not far apart in my view.

N: Jonny, the question around whether anyone can have an equal contribution is such a good one and I think the problem it represents is connected to how a group is structured. It's not an unresolvable problem, it just needs some tinkering. How do you manage incredibly diverse visions and talents and avoid everyone feeling disappointed and frustrated? Better still, how do you harvest synergy and tap into the power of the 'hive mind'? Steer the collective energies of the group positively and move them away from auto-destruction and cannibalism. I'll use Vaux and 'font fascism' to shake out some of those points.

At the time, everyone was pulling exciting stuff from their own milieus. A great example was John introducing 'emergence' to the group. I was reacting to my own habitat. Graphic design was plundering the modernist canon and it was important to show that we had some sort of handle on this. It was a form of 'phatic' communication where cues and gestures reveal you to be part of a particular club. Classic 'medium is the message' stuff. The range-left, closely kerned Helvetica and limited colour palettes were part of our liturgical arsenal – I still have the Concrete Liturgies flyer signed by Peter Saville.

At the time, the design strategy was known only to myself, and no one else would have been allowed to tinker with the Vaux visual DNA. Reflecting on it now, to our own detriment. With regards to the visual identity, I know I would have preferred a top-down, hierarchical model.

Now, like many of us, I was deeply influenced by the Nine O'Clock Service. If only Vaux could have had five art departments, all generating work for the service. This is why I favoured an agency model of production, imported from my professional context: take the kind of structures and creative rhythms that operate in a design company and use them within the group. Essentially, the final say resides with the art director.

An 'art direction' model is one way of doing things, but I don't think it fits comfortably with the notion of church or with our current zeitgeist.

I think the dichotomy of everyone being involved can be solved, and in a way where all parties are happy. There should be less frustration all round, as those who have an aptitude or talent don't feel the work is suffering either conceptually or aesthetically, and anyone can contribute and take part in the creative process; there is less exclusion.

The Vaux 'Helvetica' thing was awkward for two reasons. At the time, I couldn't envisage any other way of achieving the required outcome and it also comes straight out of modernism. Hence, it is steeped in control. However, this was before I'd heard about genetic algorithms that have mimicked design vernaculars and I'd come across the idea of 'metadesign'. Essentially, simple rules-based systems and a little automation could allow anyone to bang out competent Swiss modernism. Yet this is not the point, and a metadesign or curatorial approach would have been better.

Metadesign is 'beyond design', or the notion that design methodologies can be applied to problems outside of the discipline's usual remit. A good example of this might be the idea of 'designing out' crime. Another one might be the alt worship project, where a broken church could be re-designed.

If we were to do Vaux again, my design input would have moved back from the coalface – it would have a lightness of touch or utilize metadesign. For a start, if we were to have a visual identity at all, and this is debatable, I would explore bottom-up, self-organizing methods to achieve it. The identity would be driven from the pulse of the group. Hence the group's practices and rhythms would build it, the aesthetic and implementation would appear from below and would not be imposed from above (Helvetica). Ants, termites and wasps build very complex structures from simple, rule-based, repetitive action – why not a church? Design energies would be focused on creating systems that allow other people to design. It's a subtle reorganization of the design matrix.

To require this to happen, it's obviously a method that the whole group would have to agree upon – hence there needs to be transparency and clear communication. Also the group needs to be very flat – a collective and not an agency, a network not a hierarchy.

J: I like where you are going. We have sometimes addressed this by trying to put someone experienced in a team with a newer curator. Whenever something hasn't worked well or has grated we have discussed it as lightly as possible at a debrief, valuing the people but also trying to learn together. Sometimes it simply comes down to the aesthetic and taste, about which there is a difference of opinion. But in practice we have a very high value on permission – if you want to do something, get involved, volunteer. Ideas may get filtered by the creative team with the steer of the curator. But we trust that process. If you really want to shape something, offer to curate – we haven't turned anyone down yet. If something fails, it's probably a good disruption anyway. Structurally, in the community, we have fallen back on values or what we term 'ethos', which for us is around four words: creativity, participation, risk and engagement. If there is an issue or a clash or an argument, it's this ethos that we have let shape us. So participation as a value comes into play. Does that make sense? But it will probably always be a tension. I think it's an issue in worship curation that isn't there in the art world in the same way. There you are either curating one artist or a group of artists whom you have chosen or know and trust. I realize that there are some interactive public participation events that may stray into the same territory at times? But it's not a feature in stuff I have read on curation elsewhere.

So do you think you might ever get back into something like Vaux again with this different approach? Will the ideas have legs?

N: Yes, I would like to test those ideas, as it's the real deal. Not sure when, though. The bottom-up, self-organizing approach to design does really interest me. I'm still trying to find ways to deploy this – both theoretically and practically.

Re limits of the edge, to quote from a blog post of mine (Haunted Geographies 92):

> In the early Noughties I was part of a creative organism known as Vaux, a chaotic and 'raggedy-arsed' bunch of writers, artists, designers, djs and social entrepreneurs. The project was essentially an exercise in open source theology – a monthly site of exchange where the group learned through 'doing'. Roaming Babel's ground zero, Vaux would hang its parasitic web from whatever was available. Christianity provided the exo-skeleton, both physically and conceptually. It became a resource, a vast playground to re-pattern faith. The swarm bored through the body, riddling it with a thousand flight holes and stigmata.

Not sure if you can have an 'outside' these days, especially when one is talking about networks. We require a new metaphysics that ditches transcendence. If anything, Vaux was a 'trace' of the institution we were in critique with. I think that was inevitable. It's the same way Marx is considered to be obsessed with capitalism, and more of a capitalist than bankers!

I think you're dead right, we are all about mutating the canon, faith re-patterning. Last thing, I do think the death of the author idea (DOA) is profoundly relevant and difficult to accept. I know that culturally it has been debunked and superseded, yet I think that it makes a great deal of sense when we talk about curation, networks in constant flux and swarm-authorship. Although not annihilating authorial intent, it definitely collapses it and reduces it to just another component within the creative machine. We are not as important as we like to think we are.

I really buy into DOA particularly with regards to curation and co-authoring. We need to start to talk about distributed forms of meaning and making. Here, powerful 'non-human' relational forces like 'context' and 'use' come into play. Duchamp's seminal act of harnessing the gallery space to reconfigure an everyday object like the urinal is a good example of the power of context. Iain Borden's description of a skater performing a rail-slide is a great example of the power of 'use' to rewrite the intent of the architect.[3] Parkour would work here too.[4]

I think the initial idea of a 'curatorial' model of worship is fantastic and a fertile vein of exploration. However, it probably fits within a larger framework of networks.

J: I don't totally buy the idea of the death of the author – I like it but it's overplayed. I am familiar with the various production/text/audience location of meanings. And I like the swing to audience away from author or production but I think meaning lies in some sort of negotiation or space or relation between them all. In worship spaces I'm sure that people have read off very different meanings from what was intended – and that is exciting. It's also a challenge because I think we sometimes assume that people are coming with a certain amount of theological capital that simply may not be there! Curating is about making a world and being involved in articulation. It needs multi-valence, openness and so on, but there is still something being articulated – I don't buy the death of all of that. And I don't think I want to. We did an Easter vigil, and the articulation of resurrection in the face of the powers of darkness articulates something wonderful; it makes a world that is counter to the dominant consciousness, a counter-imagination, another way of seeing and being.

Another area that you have both talked about is those serendipitous moments of breakthrough, or spine-tingling, or being choked. Put another way, how is God, the Divine, the breath of the Spirit, the life of God, encountered or mediated in these moments? What does encounter mean? Is that what happens? I have sometimes talked about ritual being a window through which the Spirit seems to blow. It's transformative, for me at least. I remember one of those moments in Vaux when the UV lights were turned on after people had drawn journeys on a huge map of London, and as a reflection was read on the presence of Christ I was choked to see such a powerful world of Christ in the city in front of my eyes. Do you have thoughts on what is going on there? And what is the curation role in relation to it? Do we create the space and hope this gentle presence swerves into it?

K: I think that what is happening in those moments, like looking at the ultraviolet map over London, is that perhaps the Spirit is both making us conscious of something and raising us above the natural immediacy of what we are seeing to something deeper. In those moments we see both the wound and the possibility of healing.[5]

Sartre[6] puts it in a different way: who we are is a paradox of facticity and transcendence. There is no doubt that what I do makes up something of who I am . . . but not everything: we are human beings precisely because we are *not* just the sum of our actions, but similarly we are human beings because we are not just pure transcendence. It is within the paradox, the dialogue between those two states, that our humanity is formed. Connecting this back, it is the Spirit that makes us aware of our facticity – conscious of the sort of person we are and the nature of the reality we inhabit. But it is that same Spirit that moves us beyond that facticity into a transcendent place too.

Now, in terms of worship, I'd say that the best stuff negotiates that paradox of facticity and transcendence without allowing it to collapse on either side. It makes people conscious of reality, but then moves them beyond that too. Collapse into facticity and it's just boring statements. Collapse into pure transcendence and it's not grounded. So the map is a perfect example. Here was a very familiar image, a map of London, which we were made re-aware of. Pure facticity. But then the addition of the UV layer on top of that took it to a transcendent place. It moved something that was familiar into a new space, and that's where the power of it was located.

How does that work in planning? I'm not sure you can formalize that. I think it could destroy things to try to conjure that in each situation. But what we could perhaps say is that those involved ought to be helped to become conscious of the importance of grounding worship, and making it transcendent too. That's what Vaux did well, I think – we used stuff that was 'dirty', urban banality, and lifted it up a little. And I think we touched on the idea of the wound as its own healing too, without knowing it.

J: Forgive my cheek, but your reply reminds me of an incident in our shared history. I was co-ordinating the worship for Greenbelt and asked you for a write-up on what Vaux were doing, which was called Sine. You wrote a reply and I suggested that it was a bit hard to fathom, pretentious even, and asked whether you could write something a bit less obscure. You said 'no', and something along the lines of not wanting to dumb down and yes, pretentious all the way! I'm not saying that I don't understand your reply but I have read it about four times to wrap my head around what you are saying. Art can't be too direct or it's quickly boring – collapses into facticity. I see that. Is that a particularly evangelical problem? Is church and worship too dumbed down? I think that it probably is in a lot of places. It can feel very childish or adolescent. If you've been around a while there's not much in the way of depth.

One of the instincts I have loved in alternative worship is using the building blocks of everyday life and culture for worship. This does two things: brings the real world into church and enables God to be relocated back in the everyday. This adds to the potential for those moments of encounter in the worship and the everyday, perhaps?

K: Sorry – I didn't mean to be obtuse . . . honest!

What I was trying to get at was not so much that art that is too direct collapses into facticity. It's more that good art that is well curated will carry elements of both facticity and transcendence. The London map piece was perhaps powerful because it took something familiar and, as perhaps Nic would put it, re-authored it with transcendent properties. Without the familiar image – the facticity – it would have been unapproachable, but without the transcendence it would have been no more than just a map with drawing on it.

So I think that part of the skill of curation has to be working out how to create spaces that allow this paradox/tension to exist. What the evangelical wing of the Church has tended to do – as a sweeping generalization – is to collapse the paradox into facticity: here's a set of behaviours preached in rational sermons by which you should live. And what the 'high' end of the Church has done has collapse the paradox into transcendence: it's all just beautiful mystery in language that you don't even need to understand and doesn't really need to impact your day-to-day life. Both need to learn something from one another, and this is why it's been so interesting seeing alternative worship stuff – which really began out of the charismatic evangelical set – move towards the higher, transcendent place.

Linking this to what you say about 'curating beyond the canon', one might say that Serrano's 'Piss Christ'[7] was a fantastic example of someone treading a perfect line between facticity – a plain and familiar object – and transcendence – re-authoring it in a new and challenging place. So yes, perhaps the paradox and challenge comes from movement into the 'dirty place' – curating beyond the canon, curator as trickster. This was always something Vaux was interested in, though we didn't always get right.

J: What do you mean by transcendence?

K: I think that the way I want to use transcendence is in the 'beyond description' sense that Sartre and Žižek use it. For example, no matter how long a list of things we might write about Nic – his family background, the places he's lived, the relationships he's had – there is still an 'abyss' in which his person exists. (Actually, this is something that fascinates me about people's addiction to social networks – constantly thinking that they'll reach the depths of that abyss and cast full light on it, without realizing that they can't.)

N: Curate, curate, curate . . .

Digging deep wells

SUE WALLACE

―――――――•◆•――――――

Jonny: I have been thinking about curation in relation to worship.

Sue: I think this whole curation idea is fascinating. The way I see it, there have been two schools of thought here. The emerging school of thought says that 'the priest is the posse' and no one, in theory, should be in charge (apart from God). And yet in practice, what actually seems to happen is that things need to get done and so leadership emerges by default. I've been in the position of wrestling with that problem, especially in the aftermath of the public scandal that accompanied the crash of the Nine O'Clock Service in 1995. Power abuse was one of the factors that led to these terrible events. As a result I have been unhappy with heavy-handed hierarchical leadership, as we've all seen the incredible emotional damage that can happen if it goes wrong. This was one of the reasons why for a long time I was reticent to offer myself for ordination training. Thankfully, when I actually trained, I was pleasantly surprised at the focus on collaboration in ministry and the role of the ordained minister as a team leader.

Yet there is another school of thought which at first sight is in conflict with the emerging view on worship leading. A number of other liturgists believe that in worship there should be a clear 'president' or leader. The reasoning behind this is interesting, as it's about empowering others and managing creativity. Jeremy Fletcher was Precentor at York Minster when we were designing Transcendence, and he holds this view: 'I have felt for a long time that various people can lead parts of the service but I like the idea still of one person presiding (that is, with overall responsibility for the act of worship).'[1] Jeremy was around in the charismatic movement in the 1980s and believes that the only way to manage spontaneity without it descending into chaos is to have someone who is very clearly 'in charge'. He mentions the 'planned spontaneous act' that some charismatic churches used to put on their service plans. So his hierarchy is one that is geared to empowerment of others and release of their giftings within a structured worship environment, rather than one that is aimed at putting the congregation 'in their place'.

When we began Transcendence, Jeremy knew that in Visions services we passed the microphone, and he commented that it could be said that whoever had the mic at that point in time was the president. The mic was like a sign of presidency, perhaps in the way that other churches have people wearing stoles. But anyway, working within the minster environment we had to work out how to get two groups that have differing styles of leadership working together. It was an interesting problem, and one that we decided we'd have to solve through working together. Perhaps this is where the concept of curation comes in, and why I find it fascinating. A curator will plan things extremely carefully, and that planning will enable the smooth running of an exhibition. A curator will be very clearly in charge (any problems and they will be the ones who get the flack) and yet they are often completely faceless. This role seems to solve the conflict between the 'president' model and the 'priest is the posse' model. For the president does most of the work behind the scenes to enable the people to worship freely within an environment that is set up and structured to enable that to happen.

> J: You have recently been running Transcendence, a monthly worship event in York Minster. How did that come about?

S: It came about as the result of two things. One was the fact that Visions had to move into a different building for six months while our roof was being repaired. We applied to the Dean and Chapter of York Minster to see if they would allow us to hold services in their crypt, and they very kindly said 'yes'. And they said 'yes' knowing what we would do in that space, because for the past few years we had been involved in the York diocesan youth events held at York Minster on an annual basis. As part of this, we sometimes set up a worship or prayer space in the crypt, so they knew the type of equipment that would be brought into the building and how it might be used. At those events we worked with the cathedral vergers who helped us to understand the types of things that could be done in the historic building without damaging it, and what sort of constraints we would have to work under from a health and safety and a historical preservation point of view. These experiences proved invaluable when designing Transcendence.

The minster would have been happy for us to have stayed in the space, but we knew that we had to move back because we could keep equipment set up in St Cuthbert's, whereas in the minster we had to take everything down each week. Doing a full multimedia set-up more than once a month isn't feasible on a regular basis as it is simply too tiring.

The other strand to the birth of Transcendence was my MA dissertation on mission and culture. Part of my research involved asking some York residents what sort of places were spiritual to them. They mentioned the natural world, and empty churches, and especially York Minster. I also asked them what sort of music felt spiritual to them. They mentioned ambient music, gospel music, classical music and plainchant. I had the good fortune to have Robert Warren as my supervisor for the dissertation, who told me about the impact that the very first Nine O'Clock Service communion had back in the late 1980s. Apparently, although most people were talking about the dance service, which used heavy dance music within a strongly visual surrounding environment, it was at the communion service where the most people actually became Christians. They came into the space and were completely blown away by the awesome presence of God within an atmosphere, which, while it was multimedia, was also geared up to create a sense of awe and wonder, using Latin, plainchant, synthesizer pads, dozens of candles, darkness, light and smoke. Having all this at the back of my mind, I went to see some of the minster canons, and chatted about the possibility of creating something new together. Rather than Visions simply borrowing the minster space, whatever was created would be a Fresh Expression of York Minster itself. The minster is rich in musical and liturgical talent and we are rich in technological equipment, artistic talent and skill in designing creative prayer spaces. It made sense to combine some of these skills. We decided that the project was worth pursuing, and did two trial services to see what happened. The results were mind-blowing! People were in tears because they were so moved by the worship. Plus, the numbers attending were far greater than we have ever experienced at Visions. Now, as we approach our second birthday, we seem to be getting at least 130 every month and sometimes as many as 170. This in itself has led to interesting logistical problems. Structuring creative prayer activities for that number of people is difficult. Multiple copies of instructions have to be printed, and stations need to be multiplied up to try to minimize traffic jams.

J: In the art world there are various kinds of curators and contexts. Some are employed by and located in museums and have the challenge of working within old institutions, which often have great resources and treasures of art. They have to negotiate between artists, the institution and its weight of history, and the public – middlemen/middlewomen – to create something that holds together with integrity and imagination. What you're describing sounds exactly like that. You must have to negotiate in a similar sort of way to do what you do? How does that work out? What skills does it require?

S: It is true that we do indeed have to negotiate with a number of important representatives. The minster is a kind of museum as well as a living worship space, and that tension is always evident, not just in what we do but also in many other worship events that happen within the building. Tourists easily forget that it is a space for worship. They want the church to be a museum and it is busy being a church. Another example of that tension is with some of the historic chalices. The insurers would much rather these were locked away permanently, and yet the minster continues to use them – as they were made for worship and continue to be used for it.

The other aspect of this museum/worship crossover is that when we are setting up for services, we do so in what essentially is public space. It can, at busy times, feel a bit like the high street. Yet this is such a positive thing. People ask us questions like, 'Are you setting up for a concert?' and we tell them about Transcendence. Some of them come to the service as a result of these conversations, or sometimes these conversations have led on to some quite deep ones about faith and their spiritual journeys. At times I have even been asked to pray with someone. The other side of setting up in such a public space, though, is security. We have to make sure that all the equipment has been properly PAT tested for electrical safety, and that cables are not left to lie around as trip hazards. Sadly, we also have to watch over the equipment to make sure that nothing gets stolen and that we do not create dangers or fire hazards. We have to inform the minster police where we are taking items such as the incense so that they can isolate the appropriate alarms and keep an eye on that section of the space.

When we do Transcendence events we are usually given the run of the building, yet this has to be booked into the large minster diary, and everyone has to be aware of possible upcoming clashes. We have long since outgrown the crypt, and moved out into the Lady Chapel area of the church, but as exhibitions are often present in that space we then moved to the chapter house. If there are things we need such as chairs, staging blocks or carpets, these too have to be requested in the diary or they may be in use in a different part of the minster or lent out to someone else. However, the head verger is very experienced and helpful, and as time has gone on I have developed more of a feel of what we may and may not be allowed to do with the minster building itself. They very rarely say 'no' to a reasonable request. If they cannot allow things to happen one way, they very often suggest a different (and better!) way in which the same results can be accomplished. For example, in the early days of the youth event I wanted to tie ropes around the large pillars in the nave to hoist a screen. I wasn't allowed to do this. Apart from damaging the pillars, it would actually have been quite a difficult task. The head verger then told me about the hooks with strings upon them that are already wedged within those pillars. All we had to do was tie screens to the strings and hoist them like a pair of curtains. The task didn't even require a ladder and was much easier than I'd previously envisaged. So, at times, things are actually easier when a larger team of people is involved.

J: It sounds like patience and building trust has paid off for you. I do think the issue of trust is key. If you can establish that, then life becomes a whole lot easier. Are you trusted more now you're ordained, I wonder, in those circles?

S: Yes, I think I am. Some of the trust was built aside from ordination, simply by working with the minster staff over a number of years, which meant that when I was finally ordained in the minster I had a lot of friends there smiling at me as I processed by. So, with some people it doesn't matter, but with others it matters more, and often I think it's not necessarily the fact that I'm a priest, more the fact that I'm obviously a trustworthy person having been through all the selection processes.

J: How does the actual planning process work, with this team from Visions and the minster, and the two different cultures? Is there a team that meets regularly where the creative ideas flow? Or do you plan and create in a team in Visions and then negotiate with the cathedral? Have there been surprises in that from both groups?

S: It is a little complicated! What has made it complicated is that Visions members' diaries are free in the evening, and minster people's diaries are more likely to be free in the daytime! But yes, the latter method is basically what we have been doing. Visions have been planning all our services together in a local pub, looking at the upcoming lectionary themes and brainstorming ideas. We follow the revised common lectionary for ease of planning, and also because it gives us links with the Church in many different places and denominations around the world.

However, the big difference was that when it came to Transcendence we tended to concentrate on themes, visuals, music and creative prayer rather than fleshing out the whole service. Then we would feed those ideas into a meeting that I had with the minster people (usually the precentor). Jeremy Fletcher, who was Precentor up until recently, was on the committee that helped write *Common Worship*, and is the sort of expert who knows something well enough to suggest ways of 'playing' with it.

Yes, there have been surprises. Jeremy was actually more culturally savvy than I originally expected. I didn't expect the beatboxing during service soundchecks or the suggestion of chanting some liturgy over 'Life in Technicolor' by Coldplay. There have also been some surprises at the Visions end of things. Some ideas from Transcendence have found their way back into St Cuthbert's. A number of Visions people found that they liked playing with psalms, chanting them over dance tracks, singing different arrangements of them or drumming with them.

At the moment, though, we're a little bit 'in limbo', as we are between precentors. The precentor, by the way, is the priest-musician, who is basically in charge of liturgy and service planning at a cathedral. Precentors have to plan for many different kinds of services for many different types of people, so they need to know a lot about liturgy and music. So, in this in-between time, we end up having three lots of meetings: the Visions one, a meeting or phone call with Jeremy (who we are keeping on board as liturgical adviser), and then liaising with the minster canons and staff.

J: How do you work with the tradition and yet engage with contemporary culture? Can you reflect on your own creative process as you try to imaginatively construct the space and liturgy?

S: I once went to a Joint Liturgical Group conference on sacred space where someone made the comment that in order to construct good new liturgy, that has impact, you have to 'dig deep wells': that is, absorb, learn and take inspiration from what has happened in the past. Some people may never use what we have experienced word for word, and yet it informs their creativity and the 'shape' of what they do. Being Anglican, we are slightly more restricted than some people, and yet within that there is tremendous freedom, and a huge bank of resources available, if only we knew how to play with them. Working with a blank sheet of paper is extremely hard. Sometimes it's easier to take a piece of paper that has been written on, and rearrange that into something that seems new, but actually has roots. I think that's what we've been doing in Transcendence. Sometimes I feel like I'm raiding Granny's attic and seeing what is lying in there. What can I polish up here, what can I rearrange, and lovingly take out and use in a different context? What simply needs a spotlight shining upon it so that it makes sense? What needs to stay firmly locked in the attic? Sometimes this process is a literal one. I've been known to request items for prayer installations, and the head verger has literally fished them out of the attic.

This 'digging deep wells' process is very similar to the process our photography teacher took us through when I did A-level photography a few years back. Before we created a piece, we were encouraged to look at lots and lots of pieces by other artists, and work out what was going on with them, before starting the creative process ourselves. It really was a tremendously inspiring thing to encounter and has helped me in many ways. I think this process is important. But it's not just reading stuff, or seeing other services, that gives me inspiration, for the second part of the process is important too. I've benefited tremendously from the experience of being able to peek underneath the surface of services to see the scaffolding, to understand how something has been constructed, and from being able to remix and rearrange old things to see what comes out as a result. Then, even when I have to go back to the original, I see why things are arranged in the shape they are, and this has even helped me when I've had to do some deeply traditional services. And then, at those times when we have a blank piece of paper, our true range of options is presented to us, not just the ones we are most familiar with from whatever our past spiritual experience has been. We can go through the same process, not just with space and liturgy, but also with music, art and creative prayer, which is where galleries, concerts and clubs can sometimes help. I love taking two or three things that seem not to go together and then mashing them up and seeing what happens! For example, I am using 'Viva La Vida' by Coldplay, some autumn leaves and the collect for purity this Sunday. We never normally do the collect for purity – that prayer at the start of the communion service – even in Transcendence. But Jeremy suggested in the light of the readings that we might want to do something with it because of its words about 'cleanse the thoughts of our hearts that we may perfectly love you'. We didn't just want to use it straight – that would be boring! So we took the guitar riff from 'Viva La Vida', looped it, and we're going to chant it on one note at an appropriate point in the song, which speaks of the transitory nature of money and power. This connects to the rich young ruler, which is one of the readings. Then later, we are giving out autumn leaves, and one of the things people can do with them is place them around the altar, which will be lit in such a way that the leaves are enhanced. We're using leaves because they are beautiful but transitory, as is all our wealth and power.

J: I like this notion of deep wells. I think finding depth is an important issue. That is, depth in the tradition and, as you say, scaffolding/structures of liturgy, but I also think depth can come from how you are as a person in the world, the depth of immersion in culture, deep in faith, deep as a human being, and so on. Several curators in the art world talk of the importance of looking and looking and looking again at art. Lawrence Rinder talks about saturating himself with the experience of looking.[2] You seem to manage to combine that love of tradition and deep wells with a playfulness or an ability to hold it lightly. A contemporary metaphor for artistry that could be applied to curation would be the DJ who samples and remixes (or, as you put, it raids Granny's attic!). But I often think that works best when people genuinely love the archives, the tradition, rather than simply plundering it in the name of relevance.

S: I think you might be right there. There is something about appreciating how something ticks on a spiritual level that gives it depth and relevance. I almost put 'understanding' how something ticks there, and then I realized that actually it isn't really about understanding, as it's not 'head-stuff'. Actually it's more about 'indwelling', living with something for a little while and letting it grow on you. Most of the ancient stuff I've come across I didn't get from books, but from the living tradition. For example, we have a friend who is an Orthodox monk who has helped us see Orthodox methods of prayer 'from the inside'. Also, more recently, we've appreciated staying at places like Ampleforth Abbey and experiencing plainchant within its original context of prayer. Then, hopefully, when we take these things and 'play' with them they hold some of that resonance from being actually prayed and lived with. I like the DJ analogy, as I do love 'mashing' things up that no one has ever thought of sticking together, which is what great DJs do. Or maybe it's the worship equivalent of fusion cookery, blending recipes from different cultures.

J: Kathy Halbreich,[3] who is a curator at the Walker Museum, suggested that she wanted to change the metaphor for a museum from temple to town square. She is exploring how to magnify the ways in which visitors to the Walker can become more active participants in a series of memorable experiences based on discovering the links between art and life, as well as among multiple artistic disciplines. I found that an exciting statement and I wonder if a cathedra might take the risk of that kind of shift.

S: When we did post-ordination training sessions on worship we were given a number of quotes about worship from various learned people, and then asked to write one of our own. This is what I came up with: 'Worship is the stuff of life, the equipping for life, the connection with the Source of all Life, the transformation of all our lives. If it isn't doing that (at least to some extent) then something, somewhere is going wrong.'

Worship and life are deeply connected. One of the things I love about using elements of the world outside within the worship experience is that bridges are built between our ordinary lives and the extra-ordinary life of God. I was in Superdrug the other week, and 'Viva La Vida' was playing. It's a song about everything we have being on loan, all good things coming to an end, and God asking someone to give up something that was never really his in the first place. And as I listened there in Superdrug, I looked around and thought about that fragility, standing halfway between the wrinkle cream and the hair dye, and I worshipped the God who has given us a way out of a race against time that we can never win.

Of course, these bridges are not one-way. The beauty of a bridge is that you can cross from one side to the other in either direction, and when people come into our services they are hearing songs they might have in their own record collection at home, or have heard on the TV. Immediately the environment seems a bit less alien and a bit more friendly, and the step over the church threshold a little less daunting.

Wonder/ing in the multi-versa

ANA DRAPER

————•◆•————

Jonny: I first met you to talk about the youth work project in Kent you and Kevin were involved in. You described this labyrinth you had used with a confirmation class. It sounded both exciting and weird. It's easy to forget, now that labyrinths are so much more used, just how different an experience it was that you had created. I invited you to come and lead one at Grace and it was a fantastic evening. Can you remember how on earth you came up with the idea of pulling a labyrinth out of the store cupboard and giving it the unique shape/narrative that you did?

Ana: It all started in the context of wanting to engage with two diverse groups of young people. One group was very academic and came from upper middle-class backgrounds – went to the local public school and had big questions to ask and explore. The other group were working-class disaffected kids who were drinking, using drugs and generally hanging out on the streets. Some had convictions already and others were on the way to getting into trouble. So it was in response to this dilemma that the Labyrinth emerged. We needed to be able to meet the needs of both groups of people, each group being equal and as valid as the other. The danger would have been to focus on just one group and therefore to exclude the other from participating.

For us there were certain components that shaped the emergent creativity:

- A relational theology that looked to walk alongside and be with rather than convert.

- An understanding that we needed to be rooted in our context and not to be in a Christian production line – that is, it was less about the end product of Christianity and more about the journey we had together as we explored who God could be to us.
- An embrace of faith as doubt – if doubt is not present there is no faith!
- Worship as our whole lives – so the sacred was the ordinary and the ordinary sacred. We spoke about prayer being every speech act and conversation we had. ☺

These ideas formed and crafted together an exploration of what worship could be. We began experimenting and developed the idea of 'stations'. We were committed to being egalitarian in the way we performed worship. So everything was in the round, with TVs in the middle; no one ever spoke from the front but just took their turn with the mic, which was passed around as per the agreed order of the moments of community worship. We encouraged the young people to explore their gifts and abilities: some wrote poetry, some did the tech stuff, some painted, some sang, some powered the slide projectors, some welcomed people who were strangers, some told great stories and others performed acts of worship by creating symbols.

We tried to address power differential – the 'them and us' stuff that often happens. I sometimes think that church can seem like it is saying, à la *Animal Farm*, that 'we are all equal before God, just some are more equal than others'. So we tried to practise a way of being that was about exploration, discovery and being in the moment.

It was as we began being together, engaging in the discovery of what we could become and explored how we could connect together, that the Labyrinth emerged. It was more than a burst of creativity – it was a natural outworking of what we were discovering together about each other and about God – so I think of it as transcendent in that it was beyond what was in the moment;

it took us to a new place in which we discovered more about ourselves and who God is.

J: Your description of the exploration and discovery you engendered in the young people reminded me of a section in a curation journal where there is a discussion around the culture, perpetuated in some museums, that has very little expectation of the public engaging in dialogue and questions, simply presenting one truth, dumbing down art. I guess it's the kind of exhibition where people read the explanations on the labels of the art before even taking time to look and be with the art. The balance is all wrong.

Part of the problem is that (unfortunately) the public doesn't expect a dialogue about society, fame, multiple art markets, and parallel art worlds when they go to museums. Ironically, they don't even expect to have to grapple with aesthetics. The public expects one truth, the highest quality, and one way of thinking about an artist. This expectation was created by the art market and is supported by the major museums themselves. They create 'masterpieces and treasures' exhibitions, which decide for the viewer what great art is, without explaining why (visually), and they organize shows touting the artist-as-genius, as if 'he' (quotation marks intended) were just born that way. This dumbs down the public to believe they do not have to actively engage their own critical instincts, flex their own connoisseurship muscles. They are not given the tools to understand that they have a role in their own aesthetic and cultural development. In an art museum, ignorance is not bliss – and should not be.[1]

It reminded me of the culture of many churches – passive and dependent, presenting certainty. You could rework the quote, replacing 'museum' with 'church' and 'art' with 'worship':

Part of the problem is that (unfortunately) the public doesn't expect a dialogue about society, church, multiple theological takes, and parallel expressions of faith when they go to churches. Ironically, they don't even expect to have to grapple with thinking. The public expects one truth, the highest quality, and one way of thinking about God – and so on.

I think that there are two aspects to what you have described. One is the environment. Part of the role of curating is thinking carefully about how people will navigate the actual space in worship. You have made choices – being in the round, content around the edges, multiple places from which worship is led, symbols, visual projections. In the Labyrinth the whole experience is an incredible environment – a journey of discovery that embodies the idea of journey in the ritual. Can you say a bit more about how you see this construction of environment for worship? Then, second, the narrative of the worship is an articulation, albeit one of discovery and questioning and making room for doubt, but there is a narrative there. The narrative of the Labyrinth is quite related to some of the themes from therapy. How do you develop a style of articulating that is open and allows room, that can function at different levels for people but still has plenty to ponder? I think I have seen creative worship fall down when it tries too hard, or is too obvious, or shouts a message at you.

A: I like the reworked quote! I think that what we started to realize is that there really are no simple answers and that the multi-versa (as we would say in the therapeutic world) was the only way to engage in the spiritual journey we were on. What is right and good in one context can be bad and wrong in another – it is only in the knowing of the context that we can start to make sense of the meaning and therefore understanding of something. One of the questions we ask the young people is, 'What is good news?'

To the man that is starving, is it not food? To the blind man, is it not sight? To the homeless, is it not a home? So the good news became a relational issue: in our being with people we were able to respond in the way of Jesus Christ.

You ask about the environment – how we came to put it together in the way that we did. My sense is that it was emergent from some of the things we had started to do in the services – like the stations, having rituals that engaged the senses and helped the body to be involved in the process of worship. We had already started to put our services together in the round, so it made sense to create a round shape where people could walk, explore and connect with God. The therapeutic thinking came from my own training as a psychotherapist, and the way we explored in the voiceover is based on the idea of 'not knowing' – therefore enabling people to connect from different positions and perspectives. Again, this goes back to the fact that we had groups of very different young people with very different needs, wants, thoughts, abilities and experiences. Of course, what I realize now is that this is no different from any church setting – was it U2 that sang about us not being the same yet carrying each other? So we went for a celebration of difference and yet bringing people together in our similarities! We also asked questions that were circular – so they enabled people to explore and discover rather than take them on a linear process from 'a' to 'b'! We wanted to create an environment where people could be in a place of wonder/ing. I think that wonder and awe are connected to wondering, which is the essence of faith. We tried to enable the space to help people to be in the sacred through this type of engagement with an active and live faith.

The space had to be right and we kept trying new thoughts and ideas all the time. I remember when St Paul's said to me, 'You can't have the Labyrinth here because of the sound,' and I said, 'How about we use headphones?' They said that we could only have a limited space and not have anything outside of the actual Labyrinth – so we created a labyrinth with stations inside it.

Of course, people now can use the CDs, but we started with the written meditation and just doing it live, having some songs we created which were sung and space for silence, as well as repeats of bits of the meditation. It was always alive and responsive in the moment and yet prepared well beyond any sermon! I guess it does emulate good therapy in that no therapist goes into the room with an agenda of what is going to happen or an outcome – they join the client in exploring their concerns and in the process of discovery find ways of making sense of the story being told. Yet the CD was styled in the same way – exploring, enabling people to engage in a non-fixed-outcome way and encouraging them to bring their stories, so it connects to them in their experiences and contexts.

At the end of the Labyrinth we had a guest book in which people wrote comments. They were the most beautiful things. We never did this, but if you did some narrative analysis of what is written there, I wonder what kind of stories would be told about the transcendence that occured within the space – the new connectivity with God and others, the changes that took place on the journey made.

You talk about the culture of many churches – passive and dependent, presenting certainty. Of course, we need to recognize that for some this is what they seek and need. I am often surprised when people 'lose' their faith because they have come up with a dilemma that doesn't fit with what they believed. I wonder if they know what faith demands in the face of a life lived. The danger, it seems to me, is an all-or-nothing type spirituality that doesn't allow for anything but a fixed and stagnant spirituality. Communal worship, like all great art, needs to continue living and becoming beyond the moment of conception. Worship dominates the landscape and shapes and forms the architecture – it is a sacred canopy from which our bodies, our emotions, our intellect become intelligent and responsive to what is and what is to come. Maybe even becoming a bit more God-like? That is what we wanted to give life to in the Labyrinth and for some that is what it did/does.

J: After you left the youth work in Kent you ended up located in an Anglican church in Northwood where you have created/curated many worship experiences. This seems to have gone through seasons – working with young people, developing a community of adults, L8r, on the edge of the church, and then integrating the approach to worship back into the life of the church. Could you comment on that journey, and with hindsight, what are some of your reflections?

A: Ah, the great emerging journey. ☺ It is a thing of beauty, warts and all! There are lots of reflections of things we have discovered along the way and what we now think about the present and future in respect of how we express the sacred in our ordinary lives.

We did set up L8r – and you are right, it was full of people on the edges, although it was also full of people who wanted to ride the journey for a while. Kevin and I were talking about the fact that so many emerging groups/communities are made up largely of disaffected evangelicals – and that is true of what was L8r. Many of those in the community declared a loss of faith, although I would disagree – I think that they found faith for the first time in that they were actually able to embrace their doubt. But for many, of course, faith has to be concrete and fundamental – black and white – full of rights and wrongs. So when presented with the multi-versa everything collapses – or God just got outside of the box! What is interesting is that some from L8r have walked away from the shared Christian community of their spiritual journey, while others have gone back to the black-and-white, God-in-a-box type understanding, and others continue to engage, explore and create. So we can't say we achieved much – just a shared journey for a few years, many evenings of wine, laughter and a few tears, a few walks in the woods or swims in a lake and a monthly exploration of the month's 'shared stories' called Sacred Space. I don't want you to read this and think that there was ever an intended hierarchy of what the outcomes should be, so there is no criticism of the paths chosen following L8r – it just is and that is all it needs to be. ☺

For me, I guess there has been a shift in my thinking as I have wanted to become purposeful in my engagement and exploration of who God is and could be. My sense of the experience of being part of L8r is also the danger of things becoming introspective and individualistic. My own personality type is to be engaged and active – so the idea of reducing everything to just one journey and one story doesn't fit very well. I had a conversation with a friend recently who said I irritated him by always being active, whereas he felt that just being was enough.

Of course, at one level he is right – I have got caught up in the continuity of life, the moments and images that project realities from which I breathe and act and have my being. Yet he was really talking about the discontinued moments – they are also present and if we were to be more in the discontinued than in the continued we would discover a whole new world. This idea reminds me of music – the notes carefully crafted to delight our senses, yet we forget that it is the silence between the notes that make the music beautiful. We can get so caught up in the note following the note that we are oblivious of the silence.

This said, I have found myself responding to the young people in my church community, and in my engagement with them and from emergent conversations a whole new story has started to be told. Two years ago we started to think about the shared journey we were having, our need for community and a shared exploration of who God could be to us. From this came a monastic community called Shape. What is interesting is that there is a sense of belonging to each other, and the sharing of difficult moments or worries happens each week as we gather together. Of course, we have ritual that supports the process: for example, 'angel time', which is when we light a candle and people share a difficulty or concern or joy and light a tea light to symbolize giving these things to God. I remember one young boy saying how much he missed his dad who had left home and church after a breakdown, and the whole group shared lovely stories about his dad and said that they missed him too. We also have 'bullets', which are commitments people can make to the group. There are seven in all, and the reason they are called bullets is because the commitment made is not going to be easy and there might be some pain involved in living out the commitment the person is making. When a person takes a 'bullet' the whole community shares in this commitment, and again there are special prayers that they have written to mark the moments. The person is given a small stone with a word written on it to symbolize the commitment they have made to the group. One boy spoke about putting the stone in his back pocket so that he sat on it every day – and in the discomfort remembering the oath he had made to the life he was living,

Each member of Shape has an 'angel', who they speak to and pray with during the week. This is part of the bullet system: to be an angel you have to be willing to serve someone and to engage in their life experiences. So you see, my ability to just be is lacking – my sense is that you need both the note and the silence (or the continuity and discontinuity) and we need to practise listening and engaging with both.

One thing that has been brilliant is how our church has incorporated some of these ideas into their worship. We have two services a month which are 'all age' – we are discovering that families don't always want to be separated! In these services there is a creative process from which new liturgy is formed, new ways of praying together are shaped and the sacred stories told are often in the form of 'godly play' in which everyone can engage with the story from a place of discovery, exploration and wonder. So the things we learned at LOPE (Live On Planet Earth) are now part of the monthly worship of our church. Please don't misunderstand what I am saying – LOPE was very high tech and one service would take at least 40 hours a month to put together! So what we do now is much more ordinary – you wouldn't come to hear the music and there certainly aren't any great personality magnets – yet over a 100 people come to each service because they are active participants who are connected by the shared moments, by the exploration and wonder of discovery.

J: I love the various stages that you have been through, Ana. It's your commitment to context working out in practice. You and Kevin are the common thread. In each of these contexts (Kent, L8r, Shape, the wider Church) you are bringing creative skills and imagination to enable spaces in which people can explore and experience the sacred, wonder, moments of epiphany, and express doubt and be real about faith, which in itself builds a community of trust. And then you also help people engage in the process of creating and making themselves. Can you reflect on you as individuals? What are the instincts and skills and gifts that you have nurtured in yourselves? I think that others would love to learn from you in that way. Or let me put it another way – how do people learn to do what you do, albeit with their own unique fingerprint? I think there is particular interest in how to transition some of these skills into 'regular' church rather than very artistic multimedia environments.

A: Your question made me laugh. Of course what is normal for us is unique for others – so we don't see what we are being, it just is, and what we are is what we have become! A new youth worker started at the church last month and he was very surprised at the way I lead Shape – and I was surprised at his surprise! I would explore and ask how people understand things – explore the meaning of a theological story and concept in their real-life situations – and help them to transcend into new possibilities of self and ability and to create a symbolic process from which they can take the moment, shaped and formed, away into their future.

Kevin and I have in the years together become a team – one that often disagrees, struggles, explores, delights and supports each other in the process of our learning and changing. I guess that we both would value creativity as a divine gift that every

human being has – we are, after all, made in God's image. So
we are always in a creative process and in very different ways we
express our creative energy in our relationship with God, each
other and family, as well as the community we try to serve. So
we never seem to arrive and yet we do believe we are complete
in the moment!

I guess we are both keen to keep learning, and have an endless
curiosity that can drive people mad. The regular church bit has
been more difficult, in part because when we were L8r there was
an expectation that we would change the world, and of course that
was never going to be the case. We wanted to be small, locality-
based, distinct to our community and exploring at a pace where
we could walk together as a community – share our similarities
and differences, and from that sharing start to put together the
way we worship. We often get students from London School of
Theology on placement to Holy Trinity Church and they just
don't get it – we are not what they would define as 'Christian'
and our exploration of God they find difficult. We are seen as
heretical in that we don't tell people what to believe, and in our
non-directive approach of being with, we frustrate them.

My sense – and you will need to ask Kevin his – is that what
we started to do with LOPE so fundamentally changed us that we
can't be anything other than what we have become, and yet we
have carefully chosen our becoming. A very lovely friend of mine
recently committed suicide. In part it was a reflection of what
life had become for her and yet it was also the spiritual journey
she had experienced that shaped and formed the act of suicide.
She is not alone. We have been with many people who come out
of their church community broken, and yet I must say that
most go on, with love, grace and support, to shine. I can't say
I shine – I have too many disgraceful moments to be able to say
that – and yet there is a crack in everything: how else does the
light get through?

In the last couple of years I have been exploring the idea of
identity formation and the co-ordinate behaviours that influence

who we are and what we become. Of course, identity is made in relationship and we co-ordinate a sense of becoming through the image we see in the eyes of the other. I mentioned that in Shape one of the bullets is about 'calling' – who are we called to be and how do we know our calling? I also believe that we sometimes need to reject what we are being called to become. For me this has been true in that assumptions can be made about who I am and what I do that make me into someone I don't want to be, so I reject that calling and refuse the relational co-ordinations that formulate that identity. So it is often about resistance, and in resisting I start to explore who I want to be and what I can become. I think that much of people's mental health trauma is made up of the identity that they have passively accepted and co-ordinated with, which in turn depresses the sense of self that can shine, be whole and go on to change the world.

Now I don't know if I have answered your question! I guess what I am trying to say is that to be in a place of exploration and wonder – to reach God beyond a linear understand of God = salvation – we have to go into a meta-stability which means that we are not trying to create a balance, but to be truly open and dynamic to who God is in this time and place and what we can be and become. So we have to be at the edge of chaos, stepping gently away from stability and repetition to offer the possibility of the new.

Creating space for innovation

STEVE TAYLOR

Jonny: I don't know if I've been to worship you have curated or led, but I have enjoyed reading about your worship ideas from afar. One thing you have thought about as much as anyone I know is creating worship experiences for 'spiritual tourists' where they are – postcards, gardens and so on. What's the thinking behind that as an idea?

Steve: I had long been fascinated by the place of postcards in cafés, and how the card in itself was a creative expression. It was communicating something, evoking an experience, without even buying the advertised product. A sort of urban art form.

Then Mark Pierson showed me his Advent art cards. At Cityside (in Auckland), he had invited artists to reflect on a piece of art and he created a card with the image and reflection, what I thought of as a 'takeaway', a way to continue to relive the experience. Sort of like you buy memorabilia from a concert. So that for me became another step in the curation process – what would happen if the curator provided ways to relive the experience created. Holding the card, not having been to the Advent services, I also began to wonder what would happen if you removed the link to the church service. What could you load into an experience that was unchained from the need to be somewhere at a certain time and place – that is, a church service. I realized that a church service as a curated experience is essentially bound by time and space. But we live in a 24/7 world.

In response, for two years running we produced Pentecost/Spirit postcards – an image, some Scripture, a quote from a spiritual person and a spiritual exercise. We placed them in cafés all around our city. There were four in the series: Spirit as fire, as water, as wind, as earth's healer. No way to know what impact they had, but it was a creative highlight for me. We've also worked in Easter 'holiday' worship services, providing takeaway 'church service' kits for people to do church in their family groupings over Easter.[1] If I had time, I dream of doing this in relation to special dates like Valentine's Day or Labour weekend. Imagine if you could buy a DIY self-curated church service at your local supermarket.

I was reading for my PhD and this is how I articulated it then:

> Cohen argues for a number of types of tourist; from recreational and diversionary, through to experiential, experimental and existential. He views the latter three types as a form of spirituality he describes as a pilgrimage. Experiential 'pilgrims' search for meaning in the other as a response to feeling de-centred from the culture. Experimental pilgrims, or what Cohen calls seekers, sample different alternatives in the hope of finding meaning. Existential pilgrims have experienced a sense of rupture from their current reality and become committed to another spiritual centre.[2]

I coined the notion of funding spiritual tourists: what would it mean to be willing to offer resources, like postcards, to searchers, that might be a conversation stimulator – using ways that do not require them to be physically present with us?

For those who want some theology, for me this would be an expression of God in the world. What might it mean for us to participate with God's work, not by asking people to come to our physical curation as much as setting our resources free in our decentred context?

My caution is provided by breakfast cereal at my supermarket. You can buy a huge range, from healthy muesli to chocolate cocoa pops. I like to apply the same to a takeaway. It's up to the curator what they package in the takeaway. It need not be light and sugary, it can be muesli.

I think that there is a huge need for artistic-type collectives to rediscover the form of monasticism that did not withdraw from culture, but influenced culture through things like scriptoriums. In a digital world, we need a monasticism that curates takeaways without demanding physical connection.

> J: I know a lot of people who mean to do things like this. That is to say they are inspired by worship being decentred or in public spaces with no demand or connection back, no agenda, truly a gift in that sense, whether as exhibition, guerrilla or takeaway. But somehow not many people, or at least not enough in my view, have done this. I wonder if it's to do with energy levels. If you're part of a worshipping community that's creative, energy goes into the worship gatherings. It's by no means a bad thing – I love being part of such a community. But maybe it has a gravitational pull that's too strong. I wonder if we need to ask some people to leave! Maybe that's a bit extreme – or maybe to say don't put any energy into the church end of things. Get a team and curate for outside, give away gifts and here's a budget. What do you think? Do you experience this gravitational pull? Have you managed to divert energies in this way?

S: You are right that energy – in people, in a system, in a community – is complex. I think that status quo has huge pull. Yes, it is often boring and dying. But it is known. It is resourced. It has measurable outcomes. It is working (loyalists still turn up). It has funding! Just as a gallery can be a huge help to an artist, so we need the existing, yet to create space for innovation. The concept of mixed economy is both helpful but a potential hindrance, as the existing has people to bury and leaking roofs to fix. So the question is, how to be intentional around creativity? Here are a few thoughts.

1 Think seasonally or event-wise, which allows you to do something creative irregularly. Hence some groups use Easter,

Christmas, Pentecost. Much more interesting is to use cultural festivals, like Valentine's Day.

2 Bring like-minded people together. Sort of like an art collective. An hour in a café, an evening over red wine, and it's amazing to see energy grow. Or at Opawa, we've deliberately planted congregations – we've now got five or six 'fresh expressions' – which is about bringing 'risk-takers' together and letting them explore, without feeling the need to dot the 'i's and cross the 't's that might be needed by existing services and structures.

3 Tie your right hand. Every now and again, ban groups from doing what they do best. The resulting brainstorming can often get people out of ruts. We killed our Easter Journey interactive art installation last year. We'd done it for ten years and were known citywide for it. But the initial risk was in a rut, so we just stopped it, and waited to see what would emerge.

4 Change structures. This can be most difficult, but if you change structures you ensure lasting creativity. So, insist that pastors spend 'x' amount of time being creative and write it into job descriptions, or put some church budget into an art intern, or declare every fifth Sunday in the month is 'risk-taking'. All these sorts of things are ways of forcing a system to sustain innovation.

5 Create safe space around key people. Creative people are often sensitive, and so feedback can really knock them. So it's important to be aware of how feedback loops work.

6 Appreciate the complexity of people's gift mix. I've been thinking of this lately in terms of villagers and explorers. Some people are content and settled locally, while others want to explore beyond the boundaries. What relationship should the explorers have with the village? I think there is a crucial need for 'introducers' and 'networkers', intermediate people that connect explorers with the village, without forcing the villagers to explore or the explorers to live in the village. So, when you find an explorer, look for the networkers that will keep the explorer creative, yet connected.

J: To change tack slightly: a friend was reflecting on whether curation is a model or approach that might help thinking about the whole role of leading. I'm not a pastor, it's not my job, so I'm not that well placed to answer. But I wondered if you ever thought about your role in that way?

S: My gut says 'no'. And I'm trying to think why. I wonder if it's because I see curation as a 'space', both ritualized to ensure safety and spiritual exchange and with inputs that allow individualized interaction.

People hunger for connection, and artists are often quite precious about their work, so somehow a pastor might act as more of a spiritual guide in this mix. Often curated spaces are highly individualized. We've wrestled at Opawa with whether our curated spaces are foyers – entrances to 'church' – or signboards, simply pointing. I think we need to reflect on how we allow people to process their experiences of spiritual exchange and if there are intentional next steps/practices/resources they want to take.

So, using that analogy, I see a pastor as the 'help-desk welcomer'. When you visit an art gallery, sometimes you have questions and feel an urge to process stuff more. That for me would be a pastoral role, providing information, perhaps offering another resource (yes, at the shop! Hat tip to Pete Ward's writing at this point – liquid church as supplier of commodity. ☺

J: These are really good thoughts and very practical too. I think that others will find them helpful and inspiring. I have thought quite a lot about what leadership looks like in the new environment. Old models don't seem to play out too well. What you have described in your six suggestions makes me think that a couple of the roles you play as a leader are what I call 'environmentalist' and 'catalyst'. By environmentalist I mean that part of the role of leading is to create the environment of the community: in this case one that involves creativity, participation, risk-taking and engagement. (What is really weird is that as I am writing that

133

sentence I realize that those four values are the values of our community Grace – that's the environment we try to nurture/guard. Maybe we should collaborate some more?!) I think you are being a catalyst when you are identifying a cultural festival and pulling together a creative team or one of your five or six 'fresh expressions'. It's intentional but still quite invitational and light touch. It certainly sounds wonderful from across the other side of the world. And you've added a new metaphor which I want to think about some more: help-desk welcomer – that's a very serving picture of leadership. I think it's a really important area to think about and as you say perhaps one that gets left off the curator's or artist's list. It's probably not what energizes them.

Could you tell me about a couple of worship experiences or events that you have curated, or that have been curated by others in your community, that have really lingered in your memory? Maybe one in a worship context and one in a public space?

It's Pentecost this weekend so I hope you'll be throwing flames and setting things on fire as per usual!

S: For me, the words 'environmentalist' and 'catalyst' are certainly recurring metaphors. As environmentalist I create a space around a space. The artist has a curated space to work in, but to have that space requires a wider space, which is related to the church/organization/public. As environmentalist, I run interference, encourage risk, seek to remove impeding obstacles. It's a role I personally struggle with. In my early days I was more the creator and artist. But along the way I've begun to realize that perhaps I need to take a backward step, and that by providing an environment, others get to shine. Part of that for me was doing the PhD and becoming a pastor and realizing that I was gathering some language that helped to create environments.

In terms of catalyst, I have been really enjoying a clip of Brian Eno, speaking about the Luminous exhibition in Sydney, where he talks about great new ideas = promising ingredient + base + context + catalyst. I like that because it brings together catalyst and environmentalist: that is, the catalytic spark needs ingredients – time, frameworks, money – and a base – helpers, buildings.

Brian also talks about not genius but 'scenius' = cumulative intelligence of a lot of people = great new ideas, to plant a seed for a new way of thinking. I think this is really huge, because ultimately we are meant to be a 'body' of creatives, not a few star artists. So, as an environmentalist, part of my role is trying to help lots of people come together.

At the moment we're working on what I'm calling mission collectives, where four times a year I am trying to gather people around relationships and wine and some input. Rather than lurch from installation to installation, we work on our 'collective' intelligence. Our first one is this Saturday, where we will gather in the midst of our latest Pentecost installation. I'll fire a few quotes in and anyone interested in the creative process can come and perhaps it's another step towards 'scenius'. At the worst, it's a good night with friends.

In terms of memories: one year we blocked out the Pentecost Eve (a Saturday) and got an artist/teacher called Derek Lind to help us. He arrived with recycled aluminium cans and all these sheet metal tools – grinders, tin snips. People got given a 30-cm square bit of corrugated iron and were invited to depict their symbol of the Spirit. Cans got cut and painted, sheet metal got gouged and banged. Then we added them all together. It was memorable because it accessed a really hands-on, practical creativity, which some of the men seemed to really enjoy. The whole was greater than the individual, and this was about everyone being creative, young and old, and not the work of a great artist.

J: When I first arrived at Grace, Doug Holt was the vicar of St Mary's. He was the person who took the risk of saying that Grace could start, which was before my time. He used to come fairly regularly to Grace but would lie down on a pew, almost invisible, soaking up what happened and offer encouragement from time to time. As I have thought about it since, that was fantastic leadership – he was very secure as a person, created space, gave permission and I suspect headed off interference (I remember an 11-page letter of complaint, for example, that he dealt with). Perhaps the difference between him and you was that he had never functioned as an artist or done anything like Grace himself, so that wasn't difficult to move away from. I really hope you are a training base for some interns or placements for training pastors?!

In relation to the Brian Eno piece, I can see that for people like yourself you have base and context, and are able to produce promising ingredient and catalyst, which leads to great ideas, and I love the way you are intentional about bringing people together for the catalytic part. Grace is like that to a degree as well. The challenge we face (by we I mean the wider Church or the wider network who wants to see more of this) is around nurturing a new community where that can also take place from nothing. I think people look from outside at some communities doing this sort of artistic, creative stuff and are overwhelmed, or think they could not achieve it. So how do you help people in that scenario? It seems that there is a need to both demystify the creative part and also build up some capital locally – base, people, and ideas – so that the vision of being a body of mission creatives, or at least having a body of mission creatives in the midst of a wider body, seems somehow achievable, even if it's a way off. Reflecting on Grace in the light of your comments, I realize that for years there were just a few of us who ended up involved in nearly all the creative events. Now we have a body of creatives, which is a so much better place to be. Having an ethos around creativity and participation has been a key factor in enabling this growth, I think. So do you have any thoughts around how to help others develop this sort of body of creatives in new contexts?

S: Not really. I'm still struggling to get my head around this. At Opawa we have had artists and creatives join us for short-term stints. It was great and we are open to that continuing. We've toyed with offering art scholarships, but not yet got our head around how to do that well. I do wonder if the reproduction of resources might help. I know that in the early days of alternative worship I was pretty fundamentalist about 'create your own'. But the reality is that there is nothing new under the sun. So I do suspect that the blogging of ideas serves as a creative spark.

Perhaps we need to commission some travelling artists? I described one of our artists, Pete Majendie, recently as 'grit'. It was simply an observation that around Pete, like sand in an oyster, creativity forms. What would happen if a denomination or diocese commissioned not a youth or missions' facilitator but a travelling artist, who went around communities facilitating stuff, not by doing his or her own thing but by working with groups to produce a festival? This could be linked with parish anniversaries, or local events, so that it was outward and potentially ongoing.

I think courses are important. I do a number of intensives on mission and leadership and invariably that spins off new ideas for people. An idea I picked up from you, I think, was the use of random objects. Stimulate creativity by insisting people have to use things from a $2 shop.

J: Are you pregnant with any new ideas/dreams around curating stuff that you haven't brought to birth yet?

S: Always. ☺ I'd love to develop a Kiwi/New Zealand lectionary seasonal approach that draws far more from our local seasons.

J: You've been part of this scene for most of the time – what do you think will be carried forward into the future and what will fall away?

S: I am still surprised how often an anti-church vibe hangs around new forms of church. So I hope we get beyond kicking against the church we don't like.

I am always challenged by the work of Richard Kearney (Wake of Imagination). He surveys imagination through Western thought and challenges imagination to be both poetic and ethical. I also hope we keep taking forward a creation/incarnation theology rather than a fall/redemption. And that we keep creating for the sake of the other, especially the poor and dispossessed.

Curating uncluttered spaces

SONIA AND IAIN MAINSTONE-COTTON, CLARE BIRCH

Jonny: Can you describe one or two examples of worship spaces/experiences/services you have curated? One of the things you have been brilliant at is creating spaces that are child-friendly – how do you take that into account in the planning and designing of services?

Sonia: 'Come Home', an interactive installation, was trying to think about how God is everywhere and we got thinking about our homes, how God is there and how we can worship God in our homes. The idea was to recreate four rooms of a house, to literally recreate them. We had a bedroom, kitchen, living room and dining room. This initially started as a service which we did for ourselves in Bath and then repeated at Greenbelt. Each room had different rituals, activities, words to engage with – such as fridge poetry in the kitchen to write prayers, fair trade food and drink, and a small wallet-size commitment card to take away pledging to buy fair trade produce that week (this was around ten years ago when fair trade was not as mainstream as it is now), a confessional patchwork quilt in the bedroom where people were invited to write their confession on the patchwork squares and place them within the quilt. After doing this at two services we decided to set it up as an installation over a few days for more people to engage with it. We did this at Bath fringe art festival and at Greenbelt. It was important that the rooms felt and looked like rooms of a house, so we had a double bed, a sofa, a dining room table, and so on. People were invited to wander around the rooms, participate, read, think, pray. We hoped that they would go away having met with God and think about how God is in their homes.

'Rest' was based on the passage from Matthew 11.28, 'are you tired, worn out, come to me and get away with me' (cf. *The Message*). We did this as a service for Sanctuary, then ran it at Greenbelt this year and also had parts of it left up as an installation. The service was based around the idea of a garden being a place of rest. We set up different parts of a garden for people to explore, with words, rituals and activities to engage with. We set up a hammock, with words nearby that encouraged people to think about taking time to stop, time to get away from the business of life. We had a pruning exercise with a large plant that needed cutting back, and with the words 'walk with me and work with me' we encouraged people to think about which areas of their life need pruning: did we need to cut away areas of our life to enable new growth? We also had a bean-planting exercise, giving people the chance to give thanks for the areas of life that are growing and for the way God provides for us.

I think that what has been important in these and many of the other services we have curated is the idea of people having the chance to participate and engage however they want. These services have an introduction and invitation to participate, then give the individual opportunity to stop, think, engage. A lot of these have been very child-friendly but I think that is part of trying to create something that is inclusive and participative. We hope that our services work on different levels. It is a bit like a good children's film – it works for children but has gags and storylines in it that appeal to adults too! Because participation is an integral part of much of the worship we have curated they often work for children. So in the Rest service a number of toddlers loved playing with the soil and filling pots while the parents sat with them and engaged with the words for themselves. In Come Home we were all moved to see an 11-year-old spend 20 minutes or so writing on leaves to put onto the family tree the names of those in his family he wanted to pray for. Neither of those activities was planned to be child-friendly but they both worked on different levels for different ages.

J: You have a sacramental theology – making connections between the presence of God and very ordinary day-to-day stuff. I really love that, particularly as often worship can seem so divorced from everyday life experience. As a community, how do you go about curating, from the process of conceiving the idea, developing it as a team, through to the event or exhibition?

Clare: A lot of our worship has been conceived and implemented by the three of us. We didn't intend to take the lead so much – it just seems to work out that way more often than not. We've had various forums for involvement in the planning process over the years and lots of different people have taken responsibility for curating individual worship services – I think we've always tried to make it clear that it is open to anyone who wants to to do that. But it defaults to us if no one else offers! Our last service, for example, was led by a woman who based it on a prayer painting retreat she had recently been on. One guy has led several services on Palestine before and after a trip there last year. These are examples of people within the community wanting to bring something they've experienced into the context of worship. One time someone brought a slideshow and asked us to work on some stations and rituals to complement it. So the content only came together on the night – we didn't meet to plan it all as a whole. And often that is the case, as time constraints for everyone mean that we can't always get together in the same room before the event.

Even when the Mainstone-Cotton/Birch triumvirate is leading worship we'll usually meet only once and spend most of that time in eating dinner, having discussion and kicking ideas around – then go away to work those ideas up individually and bring them all together on the day. Typically our conversations start with a theme – maybe suggested by the time of year, or a response to an issue within the community, or even a Scripture we want to explore. Iain is really good at provoking creative thinking, coming up with unusual angles on things. Sonia is really good at injecting the fun and hands-on interactive elements. I like doing stuff with words and finding ways to present Scripture. So together we make a good team, and there is a lot of trust – we've worked together for so long that we can allow each other space to go away and create and know that something good will come out at the end!

S: This is an interesting one and something I have been dwelling on a bit as there was a time when more people were involved but have either moved away or life circumstances have changed so they have less time available. We have a couple of challenges. Not everyone lives in Bath, which makes it more difficult to meet regularly to plan – we have some from Bristol and Bradford on Avon. And we are a small group at the moment. I guess how we have worked over the years is to try to encourage people in the group to think about their gifts and skills and how they can share these within Sanctuary, and for some people this isn't in worship events. But I guess in all the things we do you can see glimpses of the group reflected. So, even if not everyone is involved in the actual planning, we often draw their skills, ideas, interest and gifts into the body of what we are creating. It has to be sustainable.

J: When I chatted with Clare recently she was intimating that you have a key role, Iain, in pulling the event or space together and in how it is navigated. Can you say something about how you go about that?

Iain: I think there are perhaps three main strands to how I primarily contribute. The first is creativity, the idea thing. Sometimes this is hard-won, sometimes it arrives in your head like the proverbial light bulb going on. When planning worship it comes out of reflection and conversation about the text or theme. You could fill a book with explorations of how creativity works, but I think it is rooted in being able to make fresh connections between things: a spacious view of what could be possible without editing out ideas prematurely because they are too wacky or impractical.

The second thing is very closely related, but has a more analytical character. It is asking the question, 'How well does the form communicate the theme?' There has to be a good connection. But like good art, this connectedness has to be both strong and open. If it is weak it has no focus, if it is too prescriptive or closed it feels like propaganda – you can't hear your own voice in the conversation.

The third strand is how things look. Most of my working life is taken up with making things look right. So I tend to be concerned (some might say obsessed!) about making things look right. I think a lot about images, the use of space and layout, lighting, how things are presented, the way one activity flows into the next. It's worth saying, though, that our aesthetic isn't too precious. With limited time and resources what we make tends to be pulled together from what is easily to hand. We are quite low tech. But the way things look is considered, and is a very important part of the worship experience. I hope this isn't too esoteric!

J: I like your comments around how creativity works. It sounds a simple thing to make fresh connections between things but it is surprising how rare it can be. And if I think of some of the best things that we have done in Grace over the years, they could easily have been edited out early in the process if we hadn't learned to linger with the wacky and impractical. I often say to people in planning that you need to silence your group or inner 'monitor evaluators' until later in the process – those people who ask all the logistical questions and see all the reasons why something can't be done. Those people or thoughts are good to have but only beyond the ideas phase. I find that there is great energy and a lot of laughs in a group that likes to entertain those mad connections and thoughts.

When Clare and Jon (two members of the community) and I were talking about curation Jon was stressing the need for simplicity, that the best things are often stripped back and focused down. Is that your experience? In which case, is curating as much about what you leave out as what you arrange in the space?

On a different tack I was thinking about Marshall McLuhan's famous 'the medium is the message' quote. How has changing the medium of worship changed your theology, do you think?

C: I think the focused-down and stripped-back thing is true to some extent. One good discipline about having kids in worship is that you are conscious of not wanting it to go on beyond their natural attention span – so we purposely keep our services short and don't cram lots in. I think we learned early on not to be afraid of space. In the early days meeting together was very much about finding some space and peace, and that ethos has persisted even though the character of the worship has changed over the years.

I like that quote – I hadn't noted it before. I'm not sure if our theology has been changed much by the medium – I think we were fortunate as a group to have a strong sense of shared theology from the beginning! I would say that the medium has evolved as we work out our theology in a practical context. Maybe one subtle change is that in experimenting with looser and more open forms of worship we have become less dogmatic and more open to questioning and other viewpoints? Personally I think I've probably moved on the issue of creeds, for want of a better way to put it – I don't feel that it's important for everyone in the worship to believe the same thing at the same time any more. And I don't get so anxious about rituals being misinterpreted. But some of that is just about growing up, I think!

J: I have been reading several texts from curators in museums. Several make comments about space and slowing down.

Paola Antonelli says that museums are places where you are supposed to change speeds, which is a nice way of putting it.[1] Bill Viola, whose video installations I am a big fan of, has taken to producing very slowed-down pieces. He says, 'We must take time back into ourselves, let our consciousness breathe, and our cluttered minds be still and silent . . . This is what art can do and what museums can be in today's world.'[2] Or Obrist says, 'To have moments of silence and slowness are an integral part of a museum visit. At a time when the fast lane and noise dominate over the slow lane and silence, it is important to think about how to reinject slowness and silence into current museum conditions.'[3] So your instincts seem to have a close parallel in the art world!

C: Interesting thoughts. I think that there can be something of the religious experience in really amazing art spaces. And it's always interesting to me how people behave in those places. Usually there is a kind of hush about them, a collective agreement to lower the noise and movement levels. Not always, though. I remember getting 'art rage' in Paris because a bunch of American tourists were insisting on taking photos of each other in front of the Monet water lilies in the Orangerie. I don't think I was the only one irritated by their behaviour, which was out of step with the majority of visitors who were quietly appreciating the big canvases. Seems church is not the only place where we have an expectation that others should treat the space with respect.

S: I do find myself feeling increasingly irritated when I go to mainstream church by the clutteredness and busy-ness of services. I guess this is because it is quite a contrast to the way I have become used to worshipping. When we started Sanctuary one of our aims was to strip back, make the services uncluttered. This is one reason why we have a separate discussion group, away from the worship, the discussion taking the place of the sermon. I think exploring faith in this way has given me more time to reflect and

145

is helping me to slow down, not see my journey as a race but rather as a leisurely walk in the countryside. Although as I write this it makes me laugh, as so often I get told to do less! So I'm not sure I am reflecting this through my whole life! This experience has certainly helped me to realize and understand that I encounter God most when I have space, that I rarely encounter God when there is lots of talking and loud singing happening.

Currently what I think is really interesting is that in theory everything I am talking about shouldn't work with children. It seems that the current ideas about children and children's work are that it should entertain, and provide lots of things to do, and yet we have found that children can respond to things that encourage them to stop and think. Our last service was a service of prayer and painting. It lasted around 50 minutes and mostly had no speaking, just a background ambient track. It was led by written words. Attending was a small number of adults, an older teenager, our two children (aged 10 and 12) and a toddler. It worked brilliantly – the toddler was happy drawing with everyone else. Our girls said that it was the best service they had been to. I am currently really interested in a working theology and ideas of how we worship with and view children – I'm not getting very far, or at least I can't find something that I like and agree with (apart from Mark Yaconelli but that is more aimed at youth). I think that the current views of children within the church are too much that they are empty vessels to fill, or something to entertain. This goes against how often children are viewed in the secular world, and against how I work, but I am struggling to find a way or a view/theology/theory to link my thoughts to!

> J: I have increasingly come to the view that theologizing through experience is as good a way as any to do theology. Steve Bevans, leading thinker in contextual theology, puts it this way: 'First and foremost God manifests Godself to us in our everyday experience'[4] – it's what I meant when I said before that you have a sacramental view of life. And I guess

that liberation theology starts from experience (in that case of the oppressed). The Scriptures, after all, are really a series of writings where people are reflecting out of their experience. So I think that you are well placed to reflect on what is happening with children and why, and dig to find some resources, or deconstruct the theologies that don't fit your experience and remake them. I'll look forward to what you come up with. I'm reminded of Jesus' disciples' interaction with children – they seem to act like bouncers who want to filter them out and protect Jesus from them. In the end he has to rebuke them and say to let them through: 'Let the children come to me.' Maybe the Church is unwittingly acting like the disciples and filtering children out – whereas you are saying 'let them through'! I'm sure you are on to something when you say that what Mark Yaconelli has shown in research with young people can be applied more broadly.[5]

Curating worship is usually about making spaces for embodied experience, so there is a strong instinct about the value experience brings to conversation about theology, rather than seeing theology as in the realm of abstracted ideas at a head level that are then passed down intellectually. Going back to the Come Home, experiencing a reflection in worship at a dining-room table opens up thoughts through the experience of where God might be located in everyday life, in the real world as it were, when I am sitting at my dining table. I also think that theology is something done by a community, a communal practice, rather than something done by professionals and passed down to us. And that is probably something that is done communally as much in the process of creating a worship experience as it is in the actual event. So the idea you are struggling to find is something you can discover through your experience and wrestling together with the question, obviously drawing on both Scripture and tradition alongside experience.

S: I like the idea of theologizing through experience. That idea feels like it expresses where we are at and what we are doing. It also helps to fit with my own thoughts and deliberations, with the links between my work with children and my faith and how those intertwine. I had been feeling confident about my academic frameworks and structures, which are so much about developing a holistic, empowering, constructive model of adults and children working and learning together in partnership. However, over the last few months I have been deliberating with various people about a theology framework that links with my academic framework – with not much success. I like the idea of wrestling together as a community, wrestling with this challenge. Certainly the experience of trying to involve children in our worship in a real way that is authentic has not been an easy journey for us, and is still one we keep revisiting.

When a true revelation happens you're blown apart

PETE ROLLINS AND JONNY McEWEN

———◆◆◆———

Jonny: The first Ikon event I attended was at Greenbelt. On entering the space we were asked to write down on a Post-it note something that we held dear about God. I wrote the word 'grace'. Later in the service the Meister Eckhart prayer 'God rid me of God' was prayed and it was suggested that the ideas and constructions we had about God might stop us from seeing the God who is beyond our constructions. We were invited to let go of the things we had written down and I ended up nailing grace to the cross. It was actually a profound moment for me. It led me on a journey of persuading Grace, the community I am part of, that we needed to let go of the way we were doing things to create space for newness. In the same event wine was poured into a broken glass, an artist was painting a canvas and various other things took place. It was very memorable. How do you guys go about putting an Ikon event together? Where does the idea come from? They are always so interesting.

Pete: When we started out, quite often I would come along with an idea, a theological notion, something I had been reading about, and throw it out there over a few drinks in a bar and we'd begin to talk about where that led us, what imagery it conjured up. As Ikon progressed it was less about me bringing an idea and might, for example, be that someone brought a piece of art that they found interesting or something they listened to. Our first meeting is likely to reflect on what it is we want to explore.

149

Jonny McEwen: We tend to follow where the energy is, so if we've just finished an Ikon there might be something that sparks off some new conversations so one can lead to the next.

P: The first year of Ikon was definitely strongly coming in with a theological idea but now theology is often the afterthought. It's what we do once we've created a gathering and somebody says, 'What was that all about?' Then we have to find a theology that matches up to the experience we created. It's like Kierkegaard said, 'Life is lived forwards and understood backwards.'

JM: Quite often the conversation is frustrating for people who are new to our planning meetings, because we talk around subjects and across each other and hover a lot before we actually come to a moment where we go, 'That's it!' That moment might be a title, or someone says something off-hand, and we go – 'Yes, that's exactly it!' We have learned to give ourselves time to find out what it is that we want to do. Then it quite often slots into space relatively quickly after that.

> **J:** Two words I was thinking about in relation to Ikon are 'bedazzlement' and 'theodrama'. Could you say something about them? I seem to remember that the idea of bedazzlement was something you said, Pete, when faced with a sort of popular demand for you to explain what an Ikon event was about at Greenbelt festival, a discussion to unpack it. I loathed the idea of explanation in that way, preferring to leave it hanging.

P: Ikon is primarily a performative thing designed to create a response. It's not something descriptive that you sit around and discuss. It's there to short-circuit what you think, lead you in new directions, invite you into a transformation. In a sense we're trying to replicate what revelation is about. People often think that revelation is about giving information but really when a true revelation happens you're blown apart. What you thought you understood you don't understand any more and what you thought was solid all melts into air. And we want to try to create that experience.

JM: It would be counter-productive to try to make the Ikon event coherent! We have so many different understandings ourselves of what goes on. So it's better to leave it as an event and leave people in that space.

J: and theodrama . . .

P: Instead of 'theo logos' – putting theology into reason – theodrama or theo-poetics is about exploring God in a more immersive experience.

J: I thought of Ikon when I read this passage about the tendency to play it safe with art that is somehow 'good' or avoids discomfort:

Too often, art is explained and justified on the grounds that it is 'good' – that is, not just of unimpeachable quality, which, by the way, we may not all agree is true in a given instance – but that it is also 'good for you'. But some art is not really good for you. Some art does not love the art lover back. There is, in fact, a lot of art that respects the art lover, that treats him or her as an equal, as someone capable of interpreting complex ideas and feelings, but that also treats them roughly and addresses them only on the condition that the art can be nasty, that it can ask them things they don't want asked, or make them think about things they aren't in the habit of thinking about. Conservative critics have exploited this. They have characterized the art public as virtually innocent, that is to say touchy, basically immature and unsophisticated, and, therefore, unable to absorb shock or make up their minds about art for themselves. Systematically and deliberately underestimating their fellow citizens, these critics act as if the museums were forcing something tainted onto the tender and unsuspecting.[1]

Ikon definitely has a place for discomfort.

P: We've been called 'theological hooligans' before. One of the founding values that we have is the idea that so as not to offend anybody we try to offend everybody. Our desire is to provoke, to cause you to think differently, and even more so to provoke ourselves. When we sit round the table we're not pointing the finger out. We're asking, what do we take for granted, what presuppositions do we hold, what is the water that we don't see but that we are swimming within, and how do we question that and interrogate it?

JM: We're quite unaware of an audience and simply try to push our own boundaries. We're pulling the rug from under our own feet!

J: In art it is easy to underestimate the intelligence of the audience and what people bring and how they will engage with art. Ikon seems happy to have a level of complexity that people engage with.

P: We never want to patronize people but we try to create a type of parable and a parable can be read at a variety of different levels. If you come to a parable for the first time you might get something small but if you come to the same parable after a lifetime of experience you'll get something a lot deeper. So we hope that someone who walks in off the street will get something out of it, but for people who want to wrestle there is a depth there too, real treasures that can be found.

J: Good curation in exhibitions helps ask interesting and even unanswerable questions, rather than giving neat and tidy answers.

P: We are attempting to plumb the depths of Christ crucified. What I mean by that is that when Christ is on the cross he is unplugged from everything – the political arena, from God (my God, why have you forsaken me?). Christ is robbed of all answers and experiences – the tearing away of everything that he once held tightly. In Christianity God doubts God. Ikon mimics that space where we invite doubts, ambiguity and complexity and we celebrate those as part of the Christian faith.

JM: The strongest Ikon events are actually those where there is the most tension and disagreement in planning over how to approach a subject and we have had to put together an Ikon that holds that conversation and tension in it.

> J: Where in what you do is the love of God? Good curators love art. They look and look and if that's lost it's over. So I wonder if there is a parallel for you in worship?

JM: The process of putting an event together is like the worship and the event is lots of running about (at least for those involved!). Worship is a difficult word for us. I'm not sure that what we do is worship. My agenda is exploring ideas and having a space where creativity can flourish, though other people have different agendas. To presume that God gets something out of what we do is vaguely problematic, though I guess it happens despite us.

P: Ikon can't love God or look after the people who go there. We simply create an architecture or a space within which people encounter one another, and are drawn to care for those around them, to try to help people become more loving. We don't take responsibility for people's beliefs but push that back on them. But I do hope we create a space where people become more loving, which is how you express love for God.

> J: Somewhere deep down I don't quite believe what you seem to be saying! When you curate a space, the language you have used about God is to do with just encountering God in one another. But if I think of Padraig's singing or liturgy,

when he performs at Ikon events, it is language directed in love towards God in a beautiful, even mystical way. So you do have that tone or language in the midst of what you're doing.

P: Never *just*! But absolutely – traditional language I love. But Ikon is a theological discourse and space. So we're not making empirical or scientific claims when we talk about God. People have different beliefs about God but all can sing about God. As theological language we can rally behind Padraig singing 'I yearn for home' as transformative language, as about conversion even.

JM: At the last meeting we had a discussion about what our different agendas are in Ikon and they were very different – making it cool, keeping the space liminal, that what we do makes sense even if you don't believe in God. So I think that's why we're careful about the language because we need to be able to hold all of that. We try to be gentle and a lot of that religious language is even more provocative in the Northern Ireland context.

J: If I am curating I try to create the space that you are talking about but somewhere in it will be a ritual that enables people to express something to or towards God, so there is very much the intention that even where you explore ideas part of the space is that opening up towards God. It is in this sort of space that moments of epiphany take place or, dare I say, encounter.

P: My concern is that people see Ikon as influenced by the mystical tradition, but my interpretation is more that we are critiquing a certain way of approaching God and thinking about God that is divorced from our activity, our loving one another. The only true worship is in giving water to the thirsty and food to the hungry and clothes to the naked, and anything else is just window-dressing.

JM: It has been the place where I encounter God and I guess that is our intention in some points. We have some people for whom this kind of language is problematic and others for whom it is essential! So somehow we want to do something that helps us all in our spirituality, but it's not always easy.

P: We're wanting to open up the idea of God that is in the New Testament – the God in the midst of us, the God in the stranger. So I do want to see the death of a certain type of God but also the re-emergence of a different way of understanding God.

J: Can we come back to the process of curation in Ikon? How do you move from the idea you were talking about earlier to the performative event?

JM: I think we have become quite good at brainstorming and allowing anybody to say anything. Quite often it's a flippant comment that gets taken seriously, that creates a very strong idea. So there's a kind of playfulness in the way that we talk about things and it moves quickly between deep theological ideas to discussions about bouncy castles and rabbits and flying monkeys. The interplay between those different energies means that at any point anybody could literally say anything. There's usually someone who will spot the moment that becomes the central idea or hook. The discussions then start to make sense around that central idea. Until that central idea, it feels quite frustrating

J: And do you move from the ideas to the event easily? I imagine you have a lot of ideas, but if I think about the final result of, say, the 'fundamentalism' service, where it was simply five soapboxes exploring the theme and then a concluding ritual, I am guessing a lot was dropped on the way. It was beautiful because of its simplicity but I think that can be deceptive – there's a discipline involved.

P: We do nine or ten gatherings a year and each one is created from scratch, normally over four planning meetings. In the course of the first meeting, while there might be a lot of ideas some just don't come to the surface again and some ideas continue to come back. Those one or two ideas form the basis and we use the next three or four weeks to work with our musicians, poets and artists. For those who are the most involved this is our worship: it's the most exciting part, it energizes us. Some people wonder how you can keep doing it so long, but we find that it gives us energy.

JM: We do have a sort of format. We always have a gift for people to take away so at some point we ask, if this is the idea then what would the gift be? And what would the ritual be that anchors the whole thing, and the visual idea, and the four or five pieces on the way to explore the theme, and how shall we set up the room? Those are standard questions. So in an hour we'll have five things, a ritual and a gift. And there will usually be live music, liturgy and poetry in the mix.

> J: So it does have a frame. One of the things that has intrigued and surprised me about involvement in alternative worship is the power of ritual, the embodied participatory or per-formative action. Like you, if I have been involved in an event where a theme has been explored it's the ritual that is the transformative moment, that opens up a window through which the Spirit blows.

P: Ritual is central because it is the sacramental or symbolic embodiment of the ideas we're exploring. It's where we actually bring our body, our physicality, into what we're talking about and as we embody those things we are helped to reconfigure our social existence. So instead of emphasizing intellectual assent, where we are told to be more loving, kind and generous, we want to bring our entire selves into this belief, to symbolically enact these things to help transform us.

> J: Catherine Bell calls the process you are describing 'ritual mastery' – she talks of a person who has participated in

ritual in this way becoming a ritualized agent with a flexible set of schemes and strategies to take with them as they go.[2] It's truly transformative in that way.

JM: It's also a break from all the words and a chance to do something communally. In our fractured and individualized worlds, at this point we do something together. It means something beyond what we can talk about.

J: In curating you are making or imagining a world and within that there is an articulation or a telling of something. So language is involved. It's not possible to have a void. It's not possible to resist making a world.

P: We are making a strongly theological and Christological world where one would want to believe in God. The type of belief in God opened up in Christ is that in which when someone says that they believe in God they mean that they live in a certain way – a life of forgiveness and mercy and justice and love. But then, when you say that you have to ask yourself whether you really believe in God or simply aspire to believe in God. In Ikon we are all people who aspire to believe in God, if to believe in God is to create a world where there is forgiveness, love and mercy for all.

J: Is curation as a metaphor helpful for the things you do?

P: I have never thought of it like that before. But in the spirit of retroactive justification I would say that now I have talked to you I think that this is what we have always been doing!

JM: I warm to it – it's exactly what we do. We are being selective about which things we put beside each other in that curation museum idea. And quite often the difficult juxtaposition of things is one of the most disturbing things – for instance, a video of Christ on the cross accompanied by happy music from the Guinness ad. That was all we did but that was enough: that's curation – the playfulness with which we set things beside each other or separate things or turn them upside-down.

J: One of the moves in the art world is the closing of the gap between art and life. Can you move your voice into the world rather than the church?

P: I very much hope so. It's core to what we are about, which is why we use public spaces – bars, a bus, streets, galleries – trying to break down the dualism between private faith and public spaces. We are doing a pub tour, which is again bringing incendiary theology into public space.

JM: We're not trying to get people back to church, or steal people from the church and into the pub!

Atmosphere architecture and participation

LILLY LEWIN

————◆————

Jonny: What makes a great worship experience?

Lilly: In order for a worship gathering to have impact, it has to be participatory. Liturgy means 'the work of the people' and our worship gatherings should truly reflect that. This can be done in a huge variety of ways. Invite participants to create visuals, take photos, create art, or make videos to go with the theme or the Scripture of the day. Invite them to write opening and closing prayers. Encourage people in the community to write songs to listen to or to sing. Invite people with artistic gifts to paint or create something that reflects the theme. I am convinced that getting people involved in the creation process of worship is key.

If people are engaged on their own terms, then they have ownership and they are more apt to experience the presence of God. That's why I love experiential worship and believe it makes sense. Everyone gets to engage in worshipping God on their own time and in their own way. The story is told in multiple layers, not just through spoken word or in song (which many people are now bored by). Through prayer stations and multi-sensory experiences people are invited to participate in the story in some way. They can read Scripture and they are asked to become a part of the story: to think about where they might be in the story, what they might be thinking and feeling at that point, and how they might respond to the actions taking place. How they might feel or respond to what the Holy Spirit is doing in their life at present. They are also invited to do something, to

159

tangibly respond in some way. Doing an action helps us all to remember.

So in order to have a worship gathering that has impact, it must be created with the people of the community themselves using their gifts and expressing their hearts. Taking the time and making the time to use their gifts in creative ways is worth the effort. The other aspect of impactful worship involves layering.

> J: Participation, encouraging people to be creative and use their gifts, having multiple layers – leading in this way is very different from being an up-front worship leader. Can you say something more about what you mean by layered worship? And then how do you go about pulling this sort of worship together in practice? What are the skills you need as a worship curator? And how does it work with a group?

L: Art curators take the time to know the artists and they also know the audience. They take the time to discover the best way to display the art so that the people who experience the exhibition can engage with the story. So as a worship curator it's good to ask questions. What story do you want to tell? How do you want to tell it? Who are your storytellers and artists?

Curation takes a lot more time than just putting together a worship set and a talk. It is a process behind the scenes, taking place over time. Curating worship involves taking the time to learn about and know the gifts in a community, to discover who are the poets and writers, musicians, photographers, movie makers, visual artists, people with a sense of creativity and design, people with the marketing gift and gifts of hospitality who can get the word out and make people feel welcome.

The worship curator has a vision of what could happen and how to achieve the end result, then she works with the various artists to bring the pieces together to create a beautiful whole. Hanging the art then means allowing the people in the community to use their gifts. The curator brings their gifts together to tell the story and allows them to use their gifts to glorify God. As the curator, this means planning ahead, knowing ahead of time the themes and Scripture passages. Then gathering people together, inviting them to brainstorm and process the ideas and possibilities of how to tell the story and create the 'exhibition'. The process of creating worship together is worship too, and it builds community. The most important thing is to build and gather the team of artists and allow that group to have the opportunity to work and create together. In the art world you can curate solo but in my experience this isn't good practice for worship.

If you have a larger community this may mean building a palette team that then has collectives of people underneath a team artist. So a photographer team artist gathers friends who also have these gifts and they work together or individually to create what is needed for various worship gatherings. This is actually how I would work with a music artist leader and other songwriters and musicians. This doesn't mean that things cannot happen spontaneously, but better worship happens when there is an overall plan.

I tend to start with a Scripture. In our tradition we use the lectionary to begin with but then we might expand this to work with the themes of the church year. But within that there are many layers. Creating the vibe of the space, what I call 'atmosphere architecture', involves looking intentionally at what story you want to tell and using all senses to tell it. This involves the look, feel, sounds and smell of the room as people enter, considering what story is being told through a visual image or symbols or through a question written or displayed on a wall or on the floor. Lighting can be used to highlight something or create a mood. I often use music that is theme-based. If there is singing in worship, it's good to gather songwriters and poets to write songs that go with the theme of the worship gathering, or songs that reflect the ethos of the community. For contemplative prayer experiences I use instrumental music or music with a gentle lyric. This soundtrack or playlist sets the tone and provides a backdrop while participants interact with prayer stations and respond to a passage of Scripture, an art piece, a sermon or talk. Asking round the community or searching on the theme online can yield songs. These don't have to be Christian songs. So, for example, to highlight a night of worship based on the tables where Jesus sat or for a gathering that includes communion, by searching on 'table' I found a great old folksong about gathering at the banquet table, an instrumental called 'At the Kitchen Table' and Riley Armstrong's 'The Table'.

One of the areas I also like to focus on is what people will take away. We discuss this as a group of artists and create responses and interactions and takeaway symbols that help create an on-going reminder or memory or icon.

> J: One of the moves that alternative worship has made in the UK is, I think, to break down the parallel universes that exist between church and the rest of life. So the stuff of everyday life and popular culture are the building blocks for worship rather than an alternative religious culture. This move is also taking place in the art world – or at least a similar concern is shared around art making connections with real life. Is this of concern in the USA? Is there a movement trying to con-nect worship with everyday life? Has worship become detached from that?

L: Most contemporary churches in America went so far as to create spaces that aren't temples at all. They are auditoriums with big screens, theatre seats and even cup-holders. Where in the UK and Europe you still have gatherings in old stone buildings with stained glass and wooden pews, in America we threw out the stained glass and opted out of anything that looked like church. Many new churches look like warehouse stores like Walmart or Home Depot or they look like office parks with huge auditoriums and even food courts. Once the architecture told the story, and the stained glass did too. The building itself pointed to the sacred-ness of worship. So I see a 'both/and' with this . . .

Bringing in current ideas, technology and images to help tell the story and relate it to someone's real life is key – not separating sacred from secular. Yet at the same time people are hungry for beauty and spaces that reflect sacredness and tradition. People are hungry for a place to step out of the hustle of everyday life and have a chance to reflect and be still and really connect with God and other people. We had a couple in their early twenties visit our church, which is an old Catholic building with two towers and very high ceilings and stained glass. They said that they'd visited the mega churches but really loved the old building. They actually liked the old stuff because it was so different from everything else and it felt sacred to them, not just like everywhere else they go in their everyday life.

That said, we have to create worship that is accessible to people who don't know the story. Too often traditional church of all flavours assumes that everyone knows why we do what we do in the liturgy. We assume everyone has read the Bible and knows what all the stuff is about. When I create prayer experiences I don't assume that anyone knows anything.

J: What are you doing in Cincinnati now with regards to church?

L: We have a small group that we call Thinplace. One of the concepts I like is how to make or find a 'thin place' in everyday life rather than in special retreats or places of natural beauty on holiday, such as the beach or watching a sunset. How do you engage with God in a thin-place way in your everyday world? The idea of Thinplace is a Celtic one – a place where heaven and earth almost touch. Thinplace is around 8–15 people and we do a number of things. We have a journalling group who meet on a Sunday night. We usually read a psalm together, a Gospel passage or a reading from the lectionary. We read the Scripture three times and listen to it, allowing the Holy Spirit to highlight things for us, and then people go off for half an hour to reflect and write in their journal, or there are art supplies they can create with. I usually come up with three or four questions they can use, though they are, of course, free to do whatever they like. We then come back together and discuss and share thoughts and questions. At the end there is an experiential thing that ties it all together, or something to take away to reflect on the experience, and a closing prayer.

Then there is Maproom, a worship experience with stations, once a month on a Sunday night. We meet in a coffee shop right across from the University of Cincinnati campus. We set up a series of stations on a theme and people can drop in any time between 5 p.m. and 10 p.m., have coffee and dessert, and stay five minutes or five hours. We did something similar around five years ago in a church building but I like the vibe of it in this different space. And we get passers-by who are just coming in for coffee (the shop is shut on Sunday but they assume that what we are doing is just the regular café). This tends to be with a slightly different group from the journalling.

The third piece is 'art walks'. Twice a month we go to Cincinnati Art Museum, which is free, and we do a Lectio reading in the space of the museum foyer, over to one side, and then people go off for an hour in the museum on their own. Then we meet in the café over lunch to share together. We also want to move into the neighbourhood;[1] at thanksgiving we joined another small church community and gave away groceries to needy families, and hosted a Christmas party at a nearby recreation centre for local children and their parents, including games, dinner and a visit from Santa.

> J: You clearly love working with artists and creating an environ-
> ment of participation in worship. Is this because you like that
> as a person – creating/art/participating? Or is it also informed
> by a theology of worship and the Church? In other words,
> is this just a stylistic difference or an issue of taste, or is there
> something deeper for you?

L: We have had artists kicked out or ignored in the Church for too long. My sister is an amazing artist and she had a very negative experience. The first time I saw someone paint in response to a sermon I started sobbing and the question in my mind was, what would have happened if my sister had been honoured in this way in church? For me as an artist, my passion has become engaging artists such that they feel that they have a part in the kingdom, that they don't have to do their thing just on their own. That's my motivation. On theology, along with locating God in everyday life, as I mentioned above, I believe that God is a Creator who has made us creative as well, so it's natural that our whole life response is part of worship, whether that comes out in cooking or in writing or in music or whatever. Our traditions have cut that out for so long, though, elevating the mind or doctrine rather than recognizing that God can speak through what you create or the process of creating itself.

> J: How do you fuel your creative side? What do you do to put yourself in a place where your creative juices are flowing?

L: Being around other creative people is the best for me. For example, I connected and became friends with Archie Honrado in LA who really encouraged me to go to more art museums and galleries. I have gained so many ideas from this about using art in worship and outside of the church building. It's also partly why I travel all the way to Greenbelt festival whenever I get the chance, as there is such a network of groups in the UK that gather there and those people spark me. The word buzzing for me after Greenbelt this year was 'collaboration': rather than thinking too small or local, I am wondering who the other people or artists are in my city who I could collaborate with. Time is another key – having time to be fallow. If I'm too busy working I don't have any creative space to think differently or to read or to scout out what other people are doing.

> J: What are a couple of moments that stick out for you that you have been involved in curating?

L: One is a series two years ago for Advent that was a traditional worship service. It was in a group where the singing and music was tightly controlled so that the same people always did it. So I enjoyed suggesting that instead of that we mix it up more. Instead of doing a hymn, let's do a poem. Instead of using the usual singers let's find some other musicians who weren't normally involved. I found a couple of photographers whose work I used in the visual projections. We did Lectio Divina followed by discussion. It was a blast because it really ended up being the work of the people, and even though they were a group that had been together for a long time they were like – wow, we've never done this before! Doing the Maproom locally and working with a team at national conventions has also been good because I have shifted my role a bit more to helping other people to create rather than thinking I need to be doing it all.

> J: Sometimes when people visit things at a convention or conference it can feel too big to pull off. People can be intimidated even though you know from the inside it is about ideas and it feels like anyone could do it. How do you help people get over that?

L: I encourage people to build friendships first rather than being obsessed with the task – develop a sense of community out of which you can discover ideas and who is good at creating things. But I do tell people how much time this takes – a lot longer than putting together a five-song worship set – and so you have to think differently. You also have to get away from the idea of the 'worship leader', which is someone standing in front of people with a guitar or keyboard leading singing. Curating flips this round so that everyone is involved in the worship and all the pieces need to come together to make the whole. And if I am the curator you may never see me – I am not up front.

> J: Is there much of a network of practitioners in the USA? I know of a few but I'm not close enough to the context to know how much is going on.

L: There are others, of course, but I think we're newer to this way of thinking. You've been thinking, talking and doing it for 15 or 20 years. There is definitely more awareness that this creativity in worship is a possibility, that there is no box when it comes to worship!

Appendix
Grace curation practical guidelines

———————

These notes were written to give the person taking the curation role in Grace a checklist, particularly if they are new to the role. It's very pragmatic, and in some ways more to do with the project management side of things. The theoretical side of it has been explored in this book! The list is not definitive – it just represents a particular moment.

1 Facilitating planning meetings

We usually have two planning meetings set aside for planning a service, although sometimes only one is necessary if it is a simple structure. The first meeting is usually a free-flowing brainstorm, drawing out ideas and inspiration for the theme. The second one is the time when the ideas are knocked into shape for a service and responsibilities delegated for the various components. The curator chairs both of these meetings and needs to keep them focused and on track. It is also worth doing some thinking for both ahead of time, to have things to throw into the discussion for the first meeting and maybe some notions or ideas of how things might take shape before the second. Part of the curating role in the meeting is taking notes on the discussion and order of service, or asking someone else to, and then emailing them round the group.

2 Reflecting on emerging direction and content between meetings

Sometimes after the brainstorm session there is a clear idea for a service that is going to be easy to pull together. But other times the discussion may not have produced too many concrete ideas. In the latter case the curator should take the initiative to think what might help nudge the process on a bit before the second meeting. This could be emailing round some thoughts for discussion in advance, finding a few new ideas to throw into the mix, or suggesting a liturgical framework, or an idea of a genre of service, such as using stations, a café format, and so on.

3 Ensuring distillation of service order

It is crucial that by the end of the second meeting an order of service has been created, with names allocated for tasks. This must be circulated soon after the meeting. As curator it is your role to fill the gaps – the order is sometimes less than complete!

4 Ensuring allocation of tasks

There are several areas of tasks.

- *Tasks for the service order.* Hopefully the allocation of most tasks, for producing art/stations/prayers/liturgy/video and so on, will have been agreed at the second planning meeting. But it may be that there are gaps and you need to ensure that those gaps are filled. This may involve asking people who were not present at the meeting.
- *Audio.* Somebody will need to be present who knows how to run the sound (assuming there is audio required). Your role as curator is to check that someone is available who can set this up. You will also need to check that the music or songs required can be sourced.
- *Visual.* This might involve drapes, slide projectors, TVs, data projectors, video mixer, laptops. These probably won't all be necessary, but your role as curator is to decide which are required, how they will be used in the space and who will set them up and run them.
- *Café.* Ensure that someone has agreed to run the café (assuming there will be one) – get food, set it up and serve.

- *Welcoming people.* This sometimes gets overlooked, especially if setting up gets behind and there is a general sense of panic. But it is important that you ask someone to welcome people at the door. And if setting up is so behind that the service is going to start late, let people know over the sound system what is happening. At the end of the service someone should give out a notice to invite people to stay for the café.

5 Mailing round notes and service order

Once the order of service is planned, circulate it by email. You should also ideally email round the brainstorm notes after meetings one and two.

6 Checking that people are doing their tasks

Usually everyone does their tasks and creates the content and art they have agreed to do. But if there are tasks that are quite complex, these are the ones to check that they are happening.

7 Arranging cover or alternatives if someone can't deliver

If it transpires that someone is ill, unable to be at Grace, or just too busy to do what was planned, you need to rework the order of service. This means either finding someone else to do that task, or finding, or getting someone else to find, something to replace that item or activity.

8 Ensuring that the forthcoming service is advertised

There are four usual ways we advertise services:

- Email the Grace mailing list. It is helpful if you can include one or two sentences to describe, or intrigue people about, the service.
- Put it on the front page of the website. Again a few sentences or something intriguing or a visual image help in this.
- If appropriate email St Mary's to ask them to include it in the newsletter, but only if you can do it after the first planning meeting. It's too late after the second.

- Encourage members of Grace to plug it to friends and in any of their avenues of communication.

9 Oversight of setting up

On the day it is your role to have thought about how the space will be and oversee the setting up process. In my experience some of this is improvised on the day, which is fine. If particular items are required that are not always there (e.g. bread and wine and cup and plate if there is communion) you need to have ensured that someone is bringing them. It is also worth checking in advance who will be around to help set up and clear up. There have been occasions when very few people are there to set up. It is always easier if you check in advance.

10 Collecting service material afterwards for publication on website

Please collect any bits and pieces from the service for the website.

11 Collecting feedback about the service (from team or congregation) and reporting to team afterwards

We usually reflect on the service at a meeting. You can lead that, or if you prefer email round for feedback.

And finally . . .

These notes are meant to be a guideline to ensure that all bases are covered. But curation is an art we are all learning, so there are probably gaps and you may have other creative ways of facilitating the process, perhaps via other communication means. So don't let the notes hold you back. There may also be certain services that require much more planning and a different kind of process.

Notes

Introduction

1 Kasper Konig in Hans Obrist, *A Brief History of Curating* (Zurich: JRP Ringier, 2008), p. 236.
2 Thanks to Rob Lewin for the link to the piece in the *New York Times* <www.nytimes.com/2009/10/04/fashion/04curate.html>.
3 The consensus seems to be that it was Mark Pierson who first introduced the idea of curation into worship leading, which he references in both *The Prodigal Project* (with Mike Riddell and Cathy Kirkpatrick, London: SPCK, 2000) and the CD ROM *Fractals: Alternative resources for worship in the emerging culture* (Auckland: Cityside, 2003). This description is his definition in *Fractals*.
4 See <www.alternativeworship.org> and Jonny Baker, Doug Gay and Jenny Brown, *Alternative Worship* (London: SPCK, 2003).
5 Obrist, *A Brief History of Curating*.

A space for encounter

1 A reflection from Jemma Allen – see <http://exilicchaplain.wordpress.com/2009/11/08/curating-worship-2/>.
2 See <www.michaelcross.eu/morebridge2.html>.
3 Moments of epiphany is a term used by curators in the art world. See, for example, Ann D'Harnoncourt in Hans Obrist, *A Brief History of Curating* (Zurich: JRP Ringier, 2008), p. 193.
4 Mary Jane Jacob in Paula Marincola (ed.) *What Makes a Great Exhibition?* (Philadelphia: Philadelphia Exhibitions Initiative, 2006), p. 141.
5 This seems to be a recurring theme among curators. See for example Robert Storr in Marincola (ed.) *What Makes a Great Exhibition?*, p. 24.

Making a world

1 Paul O'Neill (ed.) *Curating Subjects* (Amsterdam and London: De Appel/Open Editions, 2007), p. 182.
2 Nic Hughes uses this phrase in the interview with him and Kester.

3 These three themes are suggested by Simon Sheikh as three notions that curation in the future should centre around, O'Neill (ed.) *Curating Subjects*, p. 183.

4 O'Neill (ed.) *Curating Subjects*, p. 184.

5 Thanks to Jemma Allen for this idea.

6 A phrase used by Cheryl Lawrie in her interview.

7 Pontus Hultén in Hans Obrist, *A Brief History of Curating* (Zurich: JRP Ringier, 2008), p. 37.

8 See Soren Andreasen and Lars Bang Larsen, 'The Middleman: Beginning to talk about negotiation', in O'Neill (ed.) *Curating Subjects*, pp. 20–30.

9 In Obrist, *A Brief History of Curating*, p. 116.

10 Robert Storr in Paula Marincola (ed.) *Curating Now* (Philadelphia: Philadelphia Exhibitions Initiative, 2001), p. 15.

11 In Obrist, *A Brief History of Curating*, p. 160.

12 Michael Diers in Obrist, *A Brief History of Curating*, p. 141.

13 Okwui Enwezor in O'Neill (ed.) *Curating Subjects*, p. 120.

14 For a wonderful elaboration on contextual theology in the midst of an intercontextual global theology see Stephen Bevans, *An Introduction to Doing Theology in Global Perspective* (Maryknoll: Orbis, 2009).

15 David Holeton (ed.) *Liturgical Inculturation in the Anglican Communion* (Nottingham: Grove Books, 1990).

Treating church as a design problem

1 See <www.independent.co.uk/arts-entertainment/open-wide-this-wont-hurt-a-bit-1614419.html>.

2 See <www.independent.co.uk/arts-entertainment/art/beyond-caverns-beckon-the-darkness-lit-in-pools-1601825.html>.

3 See the article referenced in note 1.

The rise of the artist-curator

1 Johannes Cladders in Hans Obrist, *A Brief History of Curating* (Zurich: JRP Ringier, 2008), p. 71.

Stumbling into something lovely

1 Some of the images and words can be found at <http://blogs.victas.uca. org.au/alternative/holy-ground-holy-city-wrap-up/>.

2 Simon Sheikh talks about articulation in Paul O'Neill (ed.) *Curating Subjects* (Amsterdam and London: De Appel/Open Editions, 2007).

3 Hans Obrist, *A Brief History of Curating* (Zurich: JRP Ringier, 2008), p. 145.

Curating in public spaces

1 Hans Obrist, *A Brief History of Curating* (Zurich: JRP Ringier, 2008), p. 27.
2 Harold Szeeman in Obrist, *A Brief History of Curating*, p. 100.

Depth a close friend but not a lover

1 Simon Sheikh in Paul O'Neill (ed.) *Curating Subjects* (Amsterdam and London: De Appel/Open Editions, 2007), p. 184.

Gifts from the edge of chaos

1 Nicholas Bourriaud, *Postproduction: Culture as Screenplay* (New York: Lukas and Sternberg, 2002).
2 Humberto Maturana and Francisco Varela, *The Tree of Knowledge* (Boston, MA: Shambhala Press, 1987).
3 Iain Borden is an architectural theorist based at the Bartlett Faculty of the Built Environment, UCL. The rail-slide example comes from his book *Skateboarding, Space and the City: Architecture and the Body* (Oxford: Berg, 2001), p. 192.
4 Parkour, also known as free running, is the art of overcoming obstacles through creative movement. It began in France and has taken off as a creative urban sport.
5 This idea comes from Slavoj Zizek and John Milbank, *The Monstrosity of Christ: Paradox or Dialetic?* (Cambridge, MA: MIT Press, 2009).
6 This is discussed in the Philosophy Bites podcast <http://philosophybites. com/2009/02/sebastian-gardner-on-jeanpaul-sartre-on-bad-faith. html>.
7 Andres Serrano is an American photographer. His 'Piss Christ' (1987) is a photograph of a small plastic crucifix submerged in a glass of the artist's urine.

Digging deep wells

1 From an email conversation.
2 In *Curating Now* 04, journal of California College of the Arts <http:// sites.cca.edu/curatingarchive/publications.html>.
3 In Paula Marincola (ed.) *Curating Now* (Philadelphia: Philadelphia Exhibitions Initiative, 2001), p. 76.

Wonder/ing in the multi-versa

1 Fred Wilson in *Curating Now* 01, journal of California College of the Arts <http://sites.cca.edu/curatingarchive/publications.html>.

Creating space for innovation

1 This is elaborated in Steve's book, *The Out of Bounds Church?* (Grand Rapids, MI: Zondervan, 2005).

2 See Erik Cohen, Nachman Ben-Yehuda and Janet Aviad, 'Recentering the world: the quest for "elective" centers in a secularized universe', *The Sociological Review* 35, no. 1, 1987.

Curating uncluttered spaces

1 In Paula Marincola (ed.) *What Makes a Great Exhibition?* (Philadelphia: Philadelphia Exhibitions Initiative, 2006), p. 86.

2 In Marincola (ed.) *What Makes a Great Exhibition?*, p. 139.

3 In Paula Marincola (ed.) *Curating Now* (Philadelphia: Philadelphia Exhibitions Initiative, 2001), p. 32.

4 Stephen Bevans, *An Introduction to Theology in Global Perspective* (Maryknoll: Orbis, 2009), p. 18.

5 Mark Yaconelli, *Contemplative Youth Ministry* (London: SPCK, 2006).

When a true revelation happens you're blown apart

1 Robert Storr in Paula Marincola (ed.) *Curating Now* (Philadelphia: Philadelphia Exhibitions Initiative, 2001), p. 16.

2 Catherine Bell, *Ritual Theory, Ritual Practice* (New York: Oxford University Press, 1992), p. 221.

Atmosphere architecture and participation

1 The phrase 'move into the neighbourhood' is from the translation of John 1.14 in *The Message*: 'The word became flesh and blood, / and moved into the neighborhood.'